THROUGH THE EYES OF *Lincoln*

· *A Modern Photographic Journey* ·

THROUGH THE EYES OF *Lincoln*

• A Modern Photographic Journey •

RON ELLIOTT
Photography by JOHN W. SNELL

Acclaim Press
MORLEY, MISSOURI

Acclaim Press
— *Your Next Great Book* —
P.O. Box 238
Morley, Missouri 63767
(573) 472-9800
www.acclaimpress.com

Designed by: Ina F. Morse
Cover Design: Emily K. Sikes
Cover Photography: John W. Snell
Photography by John W. Snell unless noted otherwise.

Library of Congress Control Number: 2007943953
ISBN-10: 0-9798802-7-0
ISBN-13: 978-0-979882-7-8

Publishing Rights:
Acclaim Press, Inc.

First Printing 2008
Printed in the United States of America

0 9 8 7 6 5 4 3 2 1

CONTENTS

DEDICATION

To the ladies who make it all worthwhile:

Carol Guthrie Elliott
Anne Ford Snell
Jessica Elliott Wells

PREFACES

When my publisher suggested this project, I wondered aloud, "What's to write about Lincoln that hasn't already been said?" Little did I know! I since read somewhere that there are some 6,000 books in print concerning our 16th President. So, what did I find to write about and why make it 6,001?

Even a cursory examination of these pages will show you the fabulous quality of John Snell's photographic work. John made a great effort and, in my view, succeeded in giving the reader an accurate view of things and places that Abraham Lincoln saw with his own eyes. From the Sinking Spring at Hodgenville, Kentucky to the unfinished Washington Monument in Washington, DC, these images are not only eye-pleasers but emotion evokers as well. Beyond question, John's work sets this book apart from all others.

What did I find to write about? A great deal. Early in the project, I stumbled across a legal file which had "disappeared" from the Fayette County, Kentucky court house some eighty-five years ago. It was a significant find in that the file contained a four-page document in Lincoln's handwriting and signed by him disputing the questioning of his integrity. The case, while not totally unknown, is unique in that it's the only time in his entire life that Abe Lincoln's honesty was questioned. Holding in my hand a document that Abraham Lincoln had held in his hand in 1853 certainly made me know that man who inspired the marble and bronze likenesses we can see actually did live and breathe, just like you and me.

Then I found that he laughed and cried, too. A Lincoln biography will tell that Abe had a baby brother, Thomas Jr., who lived but a short span while the family lived at Knob Creek, now in La Rue County, Kentucky. Lincoln himself said that he remembered praying and crying with his mother at the baby's burial. Rumors have it that Abe's father carved the initials "TL" into a triangular rock to serve as a grave marker and, in fact, that the rock disappeared decades ago. Lo and behold if I didn't find that rock and we got pictures of it! We found the gravesite, too. John and I stood where Abe Lincoln stood with his mother as we viewed the more modern marker on Thomas Jr.'s grave. In Kentucky, I found a boy skipping rocks in Knob Creek and weeping at a grave site.

I found a young man who, like all of us who enjoy language, loved puns and used his marvelous memory to retain a story appropriate for any situation, often using humor to defuse a charged atmosphere or deflect a problem. Most who spent time with Lincoln heard him say, "That

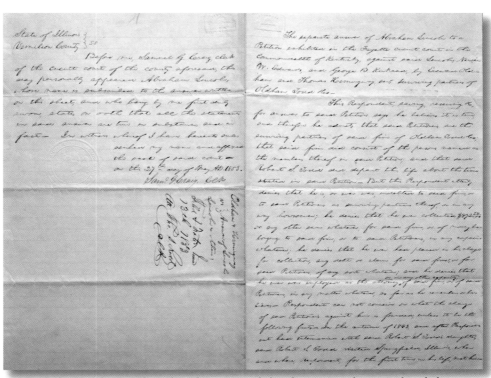

Research for this book led to the "discovery" of this fascinating but misplaced document written by Mr. Lincoln himself.

reminds me of a story …" more than any other phrase. You will find some of his stories here.

Then I began to learn how much I did not know about Abraham Lincoln. As a history buff, I thought I knew a good deal of Lincoln lore, but I was amazed at how much of it is actually true. We know, for example, that George Washington did not tell his father about chopping down a cherry tree. But that story about Lincoln reading by firelight and writing on a board? It's true. In Indiana, I found an adolescent doing just that.

Also, I discovered Abe's true attitude toward slavery. He did indeed think that slavery was a moral evil at a time that most folks – particularly those he knew best and grew up around – had the then prevailing attitude that the "peculiar institution" was simply as nature intended. Not only was he honest, he was quite courageous, too. In Illinois, I found a competent lawyer and a man of great physical and moral strength.

With no intent to write a full blown biography or a complete history of the United States during Lincoln's lifetime, the more I learned, the more challenging the selection of what to include became. You will see that I omitted most of his acts as President and Commander-in-Chief, preferring to highlight lesser-known facets. Selecting the photographs to allow you to see what he saw was a challenge, too. Likewise, I did not come to praise nor to bury Lincoln, but, as I learned more about the man, I found my admiration growing. So, to avoid heaping more laurels on him was also difficult. In Washington, I found a President who was exactly the right man for the job at the time.

Nevertheless, Abraham Lincoln was just a boy, then just a man. Of all I read, here's one of the best quotations. It's by Thomas Drummond, a Federal District Judge in Lincoln's Illinois:

"It is not necessary to claim for Mr. Lincoln attributes or qualities which he did not possess. He had enough to entitle him to the love and respect and esteem of all who knew him."

I worried needlessly about heaping on praise. To paraphrase what the man himself said at Gettysburg it is far beyond my poor power to add or detract from his legacy.

Speaking for both of us, I hope you see the man we found and that we pass along some of the emotions we felt as we stood where he stood, felt what he felt and saw through Lincoln's eyes.

Any book of this magnitude is a product of many efforts and kindnesses. We owe debts of gratitude to Carl Howell, Jr., Judy Herrick, Paula Cross, Brooks Howard, Al Boone, Emily Jackson, Matthew Terry, Cathy Snell, the Pearman family, Kenny Tabb and last but not least, Jim Prichard and Doug Sikes.

Ron Elliott, Author

Above: *Mr. Lincoln's emphatic denial of charges that he had kept money belonging to his father-in-law's firm.* **Right:** *The signature on the document shows how Mr. Lincoln preferred to sign his name.*

I was an avid reader in grade school back in the 1950's, consuming numerous books and writing reports about each in a successful quest to get a fifth grade reading award. One of those reports detailed a biography of Abraham Lincoln, my all-time favorite U.S. president. I loved his poverty-to-president story, and was especially proud that he hailed from my bluegrass home state of Kentucky.

Fast forward some fifty-odd years to 2007, when author and long time friend, Ron Elliott, asked me to take some photographs for a Lincoln book he was writing. Such an assignment would be a departure from my preference for photographing wildflowers, sunsets and waterfalls and therefore somewhat outside my comfort zone. But, realizing that this project might rekindle my childhood fascination with Mr. Lincoln, I said "yes" and we were off and running!

Our first stop was the Kentucky State Archives in Frankfort, where I photographed a Lincoln document Ron had recently discovered during his research. Next, we visited Hodgenville, site of Lincoln's birth and childhood home. Before the photographic adventure ended, we had made additional trips to the Hodgenville area, to Gentryville, Indiana (where the Lincolns moved after leaving Kentucky), to Illinois (twice), to Gettysburg, Pennsylvania and to Washington, DC.

I delighted in visiting and photographing locales relevant to Lincoln ... the picturesque Knob Creek/Rolling Fork confluence, where his father launched a raft bound for Indiana...the Ohio River site where Lincoln himself embarked by raft to New Orleans...the building on the Knox College campus in Galesburg, Illinois where one of the Lincoln-Douglas debates took place...the Arlington National Cemetery grave site of Lincoln's eldest son, Robert ... the Washington, DC church pew where our 16th president worshipped. All were intriguing!

Obtaining access to photograph Lincoln sites offered challenges, partly because some locations, such as Arlington, required special permission for photographers and because some other sites were being renovated as part of the Lincoln Bicentennial celebrations. The Hodgenville town square, site of a Lincoln statue, was being redone, so I returned weeks later to photograph the statue. Scaffolding erected to facilitate repainting the Lincoln home in Springfield, Illinois, necessitated a second trip there after the scaffolding was removed. Scaffolding also surrounded Lincoln's tomb in Springfield. And we made it under the wire at Ford's Theater the day before it was to close for 18 months of repairs.

Abraham Lincoln

After logging a few thousand miles in a quest for the pictures that appear in this book, I feel a huge sense of gratitude to those who have labored to preserve and protect the memories of the Great Emancipator. I thank Ron for inviting me to revisit history in this fashion. Thanks, also, to Acclaim Press for once more giving me a place to showcase my work. And an abundance of heartfelt gratitude goes to my wife, Anne, for her continuing encouragement of my photographic efforts.

My hope for this book is that, as you take this photographic journey through the eyes of Lincoln, it will literally bring into focus more about this man who still commands substantial admiration some two centuries later.

John W. Snell, Photographer

Relief Sculpture Panel depicting his Kentucky years on the Visitor Center at the Lincoln Boyhood National Memorial near Gentryville, Indiana.

KENTUCKY
1809 – 1816

"It was no accident that planted Lincoln on a Kentucky farm. If the Union was to be saved, it had to be a man of such an origin that should save it."

– *Mark Twain*

THE SINKING SPRING FARM 1809 - 1811
Abraham Lincoln's Birthplace

Where it is: On US 31E, 2.5 miles southeast of Hodgenville, Kentucky on the Big South Fork of Nolin Creek.

How Lincoln got there: Through the miracle of birth.

How you get there: From Elizabethtown, which is on Interstate 65, the Bluegrass Parkway and the Western Kentucky Parkway. KY 61 intersects US 31E very near the National Park.

Kentucky's recorded history goes back for quite a while as the white man first set foot in what would become the Bluegrass State some 250 years ago. For the first few decades of that period, newspapers being scarce, history recorded only those events which were remarkable in some way.

So, we have scant records of the events of the lives of Abraham and Bersheba (or Bathsheba) Lincoln–it was pronounced Linkhorn by Kentuckians of that day–who left their Shenandoah Valley farm for the Kentucky wilderness in the spring of 1782. Having heard the tales of the fertile land across the mountains, perhaps from Daniel Boone himself, in the fall of that year, the elder Abraham Lincoln settled in what was still Virginia at the time but would become Jefferson County when Kentucky became a state ten years later. History does record that in May 1786, this Abraham Lincoln was killed by native Americans while he and his eight-year-old son, Thomas, worked in the field. *That* Abraham Lincoln is buried in Long Run Cemetery near Louisville.

Thomas Lincoln was to survive to relocate with the family to what is now Washington County, which was more populous and, therefore, more secure. There, while Kentucky became a state in 1792, Tom Lincoln, uneducated and nomadic, performed his farm chores, learned the carpentry trade and husbanded his money.

By 1803 he had saved enough money to make a payment on a 230 acre farm near Elizabethtown. Three years later, he was searching for a wife. Tom took a long look at Sarah Bush – some reports say she rejected him, but at any rate, he decided on another local girl named Nancy Hanks. The Washington County clerk records that on June 12, 1806, 28 year-old Thomas Lincoln and Nancy Hanks were married at the home of her uncle, Richard Berry.

As little as is known of Thomas Lincoln's ancestry, even less is known about Nancy Hanks. Some evidence indicates that she may have been the illegitimate daughter of Lucy Hanks while other factors say she was born in wedlock before her mother became a widow. Abraham Lincoln's cousin, Dennis Hanks, always maintained that Abe's mother's name was Nancy Sparrow, the name of the family that took him in. At any rate, she was an orphan at age nine and ended up living with the Berry family near Springfield, Kentucky. Richard Berry's wife, Rachel, was a sister of Lucy Shipley who evidently married a man named Hanks, adding to the confusion. It was in the Berry household that Thomas Lincoln found and proposed to Nancy. She was aged twenty-three at her wedding and, even though Abraham Lincoln's law partner and biographer William Herndon says she was literate and taught her husband to write, that's evidently not so, as she endorsed her marriage license with an "X" while he signed his name in a shaky hand.

Today, Kentucky's Lincoln Homestead State Park is on the site of the Lincoln farm. At the park is a replica of

At the Lincoln Homestead State Park near Springfield, KY stands this reproduction of the cabin where a young Thomas lived with his widowed mother.

the cabin in which the Lincolns lived on the site and the actual Berry cabin which was moved there from its original location on the banks of the nearby Beech Fork. Some furniture made by Thomas Lincoln is on display and a bed Richard Berry made for Nancy Hanks when she, as a young girl, came to live with them.

Soon after the marriage, Thomas brought his bride back to Hardin County where he owned property. Their first child, Sarah, was nearly two years old when, in December 1808, the Lincolns agreed to pay $200 for 348 acres of rocky land in the south-central part of the county.

The newspapers of 1809 make no mention of anything remarkable happening on February 12 – indeed, the big news was that the Kentucky Legislature passed a bill prohibiting Ohio lawyers from practicing in Kentucky courts until Ohio repealed their law barring Kentucky lawyers – in what was at the time Hardin County a couple of miles south of Hodgen's Mill near the south fork of Nolin's Creek. Hence, we have no record of the weather

that day, but we do know that at that place on that day a second child, a son, was born to Thomas and Nancy Lincoln. Evidently there was nothing remarkable about the birth either, but the child, whom the proud parents named Abraham after his grandfather, was destined to become the sixteenth President of the United States and one of the most remarkable Americans of all time.

History demands that any mention of Abraham Lincoln's birth be followed by mention of the fact that fellow Kentuckian and future Confederate President Jefferson Davis was born just a few months earlier about eighty miles to the southwest of Lincoln's birthplace.

A persistent rumor around Hardin County insists that Nancy Hanks was a woman of loose morals; that she had been intimate with one Abraham Enloe (or Enlowe) and so the baby born at that time could have been Enloe's child which would explain the child's name. Those who were there say that Enloe was taller than average (as, indeed, was Nancy Hanks) and that, in his maturity, Abe Lincoln

Inside the Lincoln cabin is this corner cabinet made by Thomas.

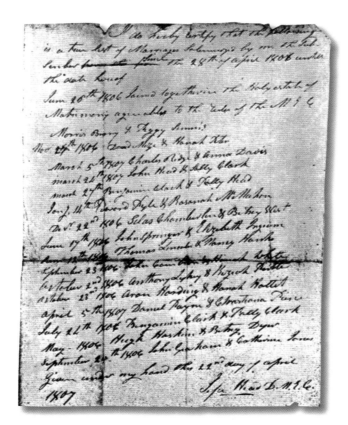

Left: This important document ends the enduring rumor, perpetuated by his detractors and unresolved even in his own research, questioning the legitimacy of Abraham Lincoln's birth as it provides the officiating minister's verification of his parent's wedding among others from the preceding week's ceremonies. Lincoln's own efforts to prove his legitimacy was unfruitful, for the document was not recorded in Hardin County, Kentucky as he thought proper but in neighboring Washington County where the wedding took place. Courtesy of Washington County, Kentucky County Court Clerk.

looked a lot like the Enloes. It is apparently a fact that Thomas Lincoln and Abe Enloe once had a fight in which Lincoln bit off the end of Enloe's nose.

Much of the controversy concerning Lincoln's parentage came about when he was nominated for the Presidency in 1860. As newspaper reporters questioned candidate Lincoln, he said that he supposed that his parents' marriage certificate would be found in the Hardin County Courthouse, both parents being dead and he being unaware that they had actually been married in Washington County. Lincoln died in 1865 not knowing the facts, as the

The Berry house where Nancy Hanks was living when she met Thomas Lincoln. This is the actual structure, moved to the Lincoln Homestead State Park from its original location on the nearby Beech Fork of the Salt River.

Thomas Lincoln proposed to Nancy Hanks in front of this fireplace inside the Berry cabin.

Above: *Nancy Hanks slept in this bed while she was living with the Berrys.* ***Opposite page:*** *Beneath the Kentucky State Capitol dome in Frankfort, Lincoln (by A. A. Weinman) stands. Fellow Kentuckian Jefferson Davis looms in the background.*

Each year as the spring recedes deeper into the rock, it's easy to see why Lincoln's birthplace is called the Sinking Spring farm.

This memorial on the hillside near Hodgenville, KY marks the approximate spot where Abraham Lincoln was born.

Washington County clerk only stumbled across the license and made its existence public in 1878.

As Kentucky politics dictated that new counties be carved out of the existing ones, the "Sinking Spring" farm where young Abe first saw the light of day is now in LaRue County and under the protection of the National Park Service (NPS) as the Lincoln Birthplace National Historic Site. A visitor can easily see why the farm was called the "Sinking Spring." The cave spring at the base of the hill, looking much as it did 200 years ago, seems – literally – to be sinking deeper into the ground. Today, that impression is accented by the fact that the spring is hemmed in by limestone rocks, mortar and concrete. It seems ironic, somehow, that although the man born here was to set many people free, his greatness and popularity had the opposite effect on the "Sinking Spring."

The hillside itself is different, too. The exact site of the cabin where Lincoln was born is unknown, but on or near the actual location is a memorial constructed of Vermont granite on the outside and Tennessee pink marble on the inside. For the Lincoln Centennial, February 12, 1909,

President Theodore Roosevelt was in Hodgenville to lay the cornerstone of the memorial. The President's only surviving son, Robert, was not in attendance that day as he reportedly abhorred the sight of the cabin. Mary Todd Lincoln's half-sister, Emilie Todd Helm, who was scheduled to sit on the speakers' platform as the guest of honor, came down from Louisville but got only as far as Hodgenville. The 72 year-old lady considered the weather that day – unseasonably warm with a drizzling rain – too bad to make the three-mile trip to the farm. Both Robert Lincoln and Emilie Helm were on hand in Hodgenville a few months later, when the A.A. Weinman statue in the town square was unveiled on May 31. Robert was ill and had to be helped from the platform while his aunt Emilie pulled the cord that lifted the United States flag covering the statue.

Enclosed in the edifice is a cabin found on the Sinking Spring farm late in the nineteenth century. That cabin was originally thought to be the actual Lincoln birthplace, but as no documentation exists to support that claim, the cabin you can see there is merely "symbolic of the Lincoln home," says the NPS. An 1895 newspaper report vows that the

LINCOLN

Lincoln cabin was carried away "piece by piece" following Lincoln's election and during the Civil War. When the cabin was returned to Kentucky, just before the ceremony, Louisville's *Courier-Journal* assured its readers that the logs were authentic. However that may be, the structure within the memorial building is probably very much like the original. Most of the cabins of that era were about sixteen feet square, but the one inside the memorial is a bit small. Perhaps it was cut down to fit inside the building. It does have a dirt floor, a stone hearth on the fireplace, one window opening and one door opening. Thomas Lincoln would have hung a rough door on leather hinges and covered the window opening with greased paper to keep out insects in the summer and an animal skin to help deflect the winter cold. The roof of the cabin is split shingles, and the chimney is of the "mud and stick" variety.

That cabin has a little history of its own. It was purchased as private property in 1894. For the next

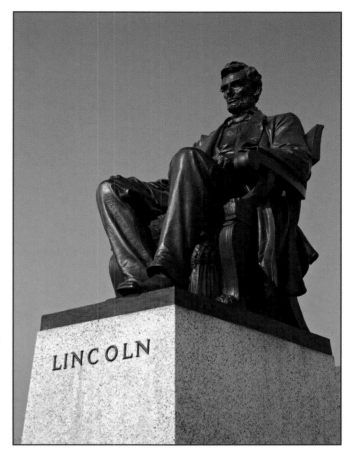

Opposite page: *Although ill, President Lincoln's son was on hand during the Lincoln centennial when this statue (also by Weinman) was placed in Hodgenville's public square in 1909.*
Above, right: *Mary Lincoln's "Little Sister," Emilie Todd Helm, also in attendance in 1909, pulled the cord that unveiled the Hodgenville statue.*
Below: Golden sunlight adds a glow to the rear of the memorial.

The Hardin County (KY) History Museum exhibits this crude door along with documentation to show that it is the original door made by Thomas Lincoln to shelter the cabin in which his son was born.

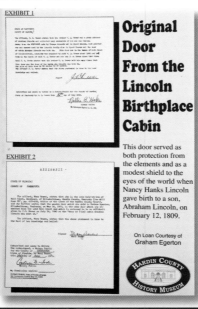

EXHIBIT 1

Original Door From the Lincoln Birthplace Cabin

EXHIBIT 2

This door served as both protection from the elements and as a modest shield to the eyes of the world when Nancy Hanks Lincoln gave birth to a son, Abraham Lincoln, on February 12, 1809.

On Loan Courtesy of Graham Egerton

decade or so, it was torn down and reassembled many times as it toured the country touted as Lincoln's birthplace. Sometimes it was exhibited along with another cabin purported to be Confederate President Jefferson Davis' birthplace. Either or both may or may not have been the genuine article, but it is fairly certain that the logs became mingled in all the dismantling and reassembling. At any rate, in 1906, several prominent Americans, including Mark Twain and William Jennings Bryan, established The Lincoln Farm Association. That group purchased the cabin and the Sinking Spring farm and helped raise the funds to build the memorial building. Two years after the cornerstone was laid, the memorial was complete with the cabin enclosed. On November 9, 1911, President William

Inside the Hodgenville memorial is this cabin once thought to be the actual Lincoln birthplace.

Thomas Lincoln. Courtesy of the Abraham Lincoln Museum of Lincoln Memorial University Harrogate, Tennessee.

Howard Taft dedicated the completed building in an elaborate ceremony. The farm, memorial and cabin became part of the National Park Service in 1916.

A longtime feature of the property was the "boundary oak." Early Kentucky deeds are notorious for stating that the property line "runs from a large oak tree leaning toward the creek," and so on. Such was the description of the Sinking Spring farm. The white oak tree in question was estimated to have been about twenty-eight years old when Abraham Lincoln was born and the NPS billed it as the "last living link to Lincoln" until it died in 1976. At the time, it was six feet in diameter at the base and about one hundred feet tall, a throwback to the huge trees that populated the country two hundred years ago.

The Lincolns' life at Sinking Spring was simple and lacking in luxuries, certainly, but not deeply rooted in poverty. Thomas farmed the land and hunted for food and worked as a carpenter to earn spending money. Nancy was more alone there than she had been in Elizabethtown – the neighbors were farther way and her husband was usually out working, leaving her alone to cook, clean and care for the children. In the summer and early fall, she would have gathered herbs and berries and picked and dried apples to supplement the meat her husband provided.

Given the skills of the couple and the necessities of the time, it is not difficult to look inside the cabin and envision toddler Sarah playing on the dirt floor while Nancy is spinning and weaving cloth in front of the hearth, her foot rocking baby Abraham in the cradle Thomas made for her.

The Lincolns were to remain at the Sinking Spring for only two years before the promise of better land lured Thomas a few miles to the northeast. Perhaps young Abe's eyes had a last glimpse of the hills and trees over his mother's shoulder as she carried him from the cabin for the last time, but he would have no memories of the place of his birth, and there is no record of his ever having visited. Nonetheless, the location is there for us to visit and enjoy as we pay homage to the man who was born in those humble surroundings.

A page from the Hardin County Court Order book appoints Thomas Lincoln, among others, as a "padroller." The duties of that office included prowling the roads to apprehend fugitive slaves. Lincoln's acceptance of the appointment gives us some insight into his feelings about slavery. Courtesy of Hardin County, Kentucky County Clerk.

LINCOLN'S BOYHOOD HOME
The Knob Creek Farm 1811-1816

Where it is: On US 31E ten miles north of the Sinking Spring Farm, between Hodgenville and New Haven.

How Lincoln Got There: In his mother's arms. Perhaps she walked from the Sinking Spring farm; maybe she rode in a wagon.

How you get there: Leaving the Lincoln birthplace, simply go north on US 31E.

Like a drunken snake, US 31E meanders its way through LaRue County's "knobs" – the low round hills that populate Central Kentucky – probably on the path chosen by the buffalo hundreds of years ago. If you leave the Lincoln Birthplace site, and drive north along it, you'll go around the statue of Lincoln in the middle of Hodgenville and then parallel the path of Knob Creek in the natural valley carved through the surrounding hills. You'll notice that here and there, fingers of land stretch back into Kentucky's famous "hollers," relatively level spots between the hills.

Thomas Lincoln agreed to purchase one such tract known at the time as Thompson's Holler, of about 230 acres and moved his family there in 1811. Very soon after the move, he sold about two hundred acres, keeping the best part of the farm.

When first seeing the thirty acres Thomas kept, one is immediately struck by the contrast between that property and the Sinking Spring farm. While the former, as a Kentuckian once noted has "two rocks for ever' dirt," the Lincoln Knob Creek location is as pleasing to the eye as any property in the area, just a beautiful grassy meadow extending from the highway back into the hills. About half of the Knob Creek farm is "bottom land," level, fertile soil bordering the creek at the base of the hills. Anyone who ever scratched in the dirt for a living knows that such land, being in the alluvial plain, is the richest farm land to be had.

The Lincoln home here was a cabin much like the one at Sinking Spring. There is such a cabin there today, the National Park Service says it belonged to the Gollahers, the family of Abraham's childhood friend. The NPS only took over management of the farm in 2001, so about all they have accomplished so far is to shore up the cabin to prevent further deterioration. This cabin has one door and one window and is full sized as it is outdoors in its original condition.

Also in contrast to the isolated Sinking Spring, this farm is right on the highway, which was the major Louisville to Nashville thoroughfare in Lincoln's day – the "main street of the Kentucky wilderness." This area being more densely settled than the Lincolns' former residence to the south, Knob Creek was a relative beehive of activity. There were neighbors to visit and neighborhood activities, such as barn raisings and quilting parties. Travelers and peddlers passing by brought news and tales of far away places and discussions of previously unknown topics. Long after Lincoln's death, much speculation has been made concerning his first exposure to the "peculiar intuition," slavery. It is probable that from the yard of the Knob Creek cabin the young Lincoln saw gangs of slaves headed south – being "sold down the river." While slavery was not nearly as prevalent in Kentucky as in the deep south, it may also be that some of the local residents owned a few slaves – there were some 1,000 slaves in Hardin County in 1811.

Near Thomas Lincoln Jr's grave site, one can see the beautiful view from atop one of LaRue County's "knobs."

The "holler" at the Knob Creek farm looks no different today from when the Lincolns' lived here. The creek is to the right in this view.

Knob Creek is just the same as it was when the boys skipped rocks during Lincoln's childhood.

Then as now, the creek is the main feature of the property. Not only did it serve as a boundary and furnish water for household use, the rushing water also nourished the crops and the abundant fauna. In the spring of the year Thomas tilled the fertile ground along the creek, a horse pulling the plow. Sarah followed, scooping the loosened soil into small hills about 12 inches apart. Young Abe, too small to be of much help, followed along dropping a pumpkin seed to every fourth hill. Finally, Nancy ended the parade, adding seed corn to the mounds, four seeds per hill. Sometimes Abraham may have heard her chant, "one to rot, one for the crow, one to die and one to grow" as she buried the seeds in the dirt. When the chore was finished, the farmers hoped for rain, so that the back-breaking chore of carrying water from the creek to nourish the seedlings would not be necessary.

But they didn't want too much rain as happened one of the years the Lincolns lived at Knob Creek. On that occasion, the planting was followed by a deluge which caused it "to come a tide" in the Knob Creek. The water overflowing the creek banks washed away the corn seed, the pumpkin seed and all the hard labor in one night. Such fickleness of nature was just part of a frontier child's education. The pioneers could only accept such events philosophically – there was simply too much work to be done to waste time fretting.

As an added bonus for Abe and his friend, the creek also provided a source of recreation for boys, who have always liked water in its natural habitat That same creek water in which the boys skipped flat stones nearly deprived the United States of Abraham Lincoln. His childhood playmate, Austin Gollaher, relates that in 1816 he saved his seven-year-old friend's life. As the boys were wandering up and down the Knob Creek, its depth rain swollen to seven or eight feet, they spotted a slender log spanning the stream. "It was narrow, but Abe said, 'Let's coon it,'" Gollaher reported many years later. Despite the fact that neither could swim, they decided to walk across the log. Gollaher went first. When he reached the far bank safely, Lincoln started across. Gollaher goes on, "… about half-

Knob Creek near the original cabin site. The water is low in this photograph, but this spot, near the cabin site, is possibly the "swimmin' hole" where Austin Gollaher saved Lincoln's life.

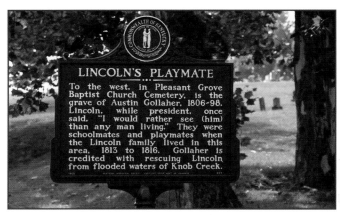

A Kentucky Historical Society plaque adorns the Pleasant Grove Baptist Church Cemetery near the Knob Creek farm.

"Aus," as Abe knew him, lived a long life entirely in LaRue County.

way across, he got scared and began trembling…then he fell off into the creek…. I knew it would do no good for me to go in after him."

Thinking quickly, Austin picked up a tree limb lying nearby. When Lincoln resurfaced, Gollaher put the stick in Abe's hands. "He clung to it and I was able to pull him to the bank, almost dead. I got him by the arms and shook him well. When I rolled him on the ground, water poured out of his mouth." Gollaher relates that for fear the parents would be angry, both boys took off their clothes to allow them to dry in the sun and swore each other to secrecy. In 1895, "Aus," as Lincoln knew him, said that he didn't think either set of parents ever learned of the adventure. Gollaher remained in the area all his days. At his death in

1898, he was buried in the Pleasant Grove Baptist Church yard near the Knob Creek farm.

About two miles farther along US 31E (North) toward New Haven is the hamlet of Athertonville, site of young Lincoln's first "formal" schooling. The school building is no longer there for us to see, but we know that it differed in some small details from the log homes. As school sessions were held only during the winter months when it was too cold for farm work, a fireplace was a fixture. A school building usually lacked any window; such an opening would serve only to allow heat to escape and distract the scholars. Like homes, log schools were one-room structures but sometimes had a log omitted near the roof of the structure for lighting and ventilation. Inside, split logs provided rough benches for the students. Accompanied by his sister, Abe walked to the two miles to Athertonville, there to study his lessons in "readin', writin' and ciperin'." All study was done aloud – how else was the teacher to know the students were actually studying? Such schools were, therefore, termed "blab schools," the only type Lincoln ever attended.

As the schools were subscription affairs, a nominal fee being charged for each student, attendance was small. Lincoln's friend and classmate, Austin Gollaher, reported about twenty students ranging in age from five to sixteen in the summer of 1815. One can only imagine the din inside the small room as twenty students simultaneously "blabbed" their lessons. Perhaps because of the "blab" idea, for the rest of his life, Lincoln always read aloud on any topic he was mulling over, much to the chagrin of those with whom he shared an office.

Lincoln attended two terms of school, each about three months at this location. His teachers were Caleb Hazel and Zachariah Riney. Riney's daughter, one of Abe's classmates, was to remember him "wearing homespun clothes, as we all did, and barefooted," and as a child of "unfailing good humor." Many years after his attendance, Lincoln himself was to say of the frontier schools, "…no qualification was ever required of a teacher beyond readin', writin' and ciperin' to the rule of three." These are, perhaps not so coincidentally, the same educational qualifications Lincoln claimed for himself, anything else having been, "picked up from time to time under the pressure of necessity." Commenting on the qualifications of teachers, he also

added that, "if a straggler supposed to understand Latin happened to sojourn in the neighborhood, he was looked upon as a wizzard (sic)."

Young Lincoln would have been old enough to take on a few chores while at Knob Creek. He probably carried water from the creek, brought in fire wood, cleaned ashes from the fireplace, hoed the corn field, picked blackberries and gathered nuts in the surrounding hills, fished the creek and perhaps ran a few errands for his father. One report exists stating that Thomas Lincoln worked in John Boone's distillery in this neighborhood and that one of his son's duties was to carry dinner to his father's work place.

While residing at Knob Creek, Abe was probably educated in the workings of the legal system as well. Thomas Lincoln was no stranger to the courtroom, having served on juries and appeared as a witness on several occasions. Also, he was the defendant in several suits, accused of unpaid debt. We tend to think that buying on credit is a modern idea, but the practice was wide-spread by 1800. In fact, there is no record of Tom Lincoln having ever made any payment on the Knob Creek farm, or the Sinking Spring place either for that matter. In addition, the elder Lincoln had to defend himself against "unworkmanlike" carpentry on a few occasions. Then, there was "court day" in the county seat, a major source of pioneer entertainment. On the first Monday of each month, judges, lawyers, and citizens would descend upon the Hardin County courthouse for the legal proceedings while vendors, cattlemen, horse and mule traders and con men would flock into Elizabethtown for the carnival-like festivities. Almost certainly, the entire Lincoln family attended Hardin County's court days, so, even if the young man did not accompany his father into the courtroom, he would certainly have been aware of the proceedings.

Another factor in every family's life in those times was possibility of infant death. One has only to visit a pioneer cemetery and observe the number of tiny graves to understand that any child who escaped smallpox, measles and the other deadly childhood maladies to survive to maturity was indeed fortunate.

An original log school building. The "blab" school Lincoln attended would have looked like this one. Note that no window prevents any possible distraction for the students.

The tragedy of infant death was visited on the Lincoln household when Thomas and Nancy's third child, a son also named Thomas, died after living only a short while. Due to scanty record keeping of those days and the child's short life span, the exact dates of birth and death are not known, in fact all that is known is from Lincoln's autobiography which simply says his younger brother "died in infancy."

The child may have been born at the Sinking Spring farm, but the fact that young Thomas' grave is just across the knob from the Knob Creek farm indicates that the baby was probably born and almost certainly died while the family was there. The grave, located in the Redmon family cemetery, was first identified when a small triangular limestone rock inscribed "TL" was discovered by a government-funded LaRue County work crew in 1933. That stone was removed from the grave site when a former owner of the property took it with him when he sold the farm. It is now in the possession

The stone placed on young Thomas' grave by the Boy Scouts of Des Moines. Weathering has rendered all the other stones in the private cemetery illegible.

Thomas Lincoln Junior's original grave stone. Legend has it that Thomas Lincoln carved his son's initials in this rock which was missing for several decades.

of Hodgenville attorney Carl Howell, Jr., who was kind enough to allow us to photograph it. The grave site, located on private property, is now marked by a stone placed there by Boy Scouts in 1959. Evidently the Des Moines Boy Scouts inscribed "1811-1815" on the marker to indicate that the child lived sometime during that time frame and got a little familiar with "Tommy." The property owners were also kind enough to allow us access to the cemetery for photographs. Most of the other stones are so weather-beaten as to be illegible, but around Hodgenville, the story is that young Thomas is the only non-Redmon buried in the plot.

The Lincolns' life at Knob Creek was as simple as at the Sinking Spring. The entire family wore linsey-woolsey clothes home spun by Nancy. Schoolmates report that Sarah and Abe both attended school wearing only a nightshirt type garment. No frills was the rule – not a pin nor a button would be found.

The Knob Creek Lincolns probably owned a cow and a calf; the duo could be had for about ten dollars which was well within Thomas' means. From early spring to late fall, the cow would be allowed to roam freely in the woods as she would voluntarily return to the farm to feed her calf at evening. Sarah would have been in charge of the milking. She would drive the cow into a corner of the rail fence, then release the calf to begin its meal. When the milk was flowing freely, Sarah would lead the protesting calf back to the pen. Not using a stool, but standing, Sarah would extract the family's share of the cow's bounty, squirting the milk into a gourd and stopping occasionally to empty the contents into a pail stashed safely out of danger of being kicked over. When the family's needs were met, the calf would be released to finish its feeding.

In addition to farming, Thomas would have hunted in the surrounding hills. The abundant buffalo, deer, wild turkey, rabbits and squirrels were easy prey and provided plenty of meat for the table. He also worked irregularly as a carpenter, sometimes in Elizabethtown, sometimes in Bardstown. Usually, he was paid in money, but occasionally he accepted his pay in wheat flour. Accustomed to nothing but cornbread, flour biscuits with butter and perhaps some wild honey would be a treat for the whole family.

Inside the house, Nancy cooked and cleaned, carded, spun and wove wool. In addition, she probably raised a vegetable garden near the cabin. In season, she would have climbed the steep hills back of the cabin to gather the abundant walnuts, hickory nuts and blackberries

Abraham's wife Mary's father, Robert Todd owned this home in Lexington, KY where the couple would visit in 1846.

and blueberries. While on such missions, perhaps she occasionally allowed herself the luxury of a bouquet of the luxuriant wildflowers to be found atop those knobs.

The Commonwealth of Virginia had paid her Revolutionary soldiers with Kentucky land warrants, issuing many more than there was land to fulfill. When coupled with the previously mentioned uncertain terminology in deeds, obtaining clear title to Kentucky land was a difficult chore. Thomas Lincoln had already had his troubles in that regard with the Sinking Spring farm, accounting for several of his court appearances. In the summer of 1816 a law suit concerning the title to the Knob Creek farm was pending, so he may have become frustrated in the attempt to gain title to the property. In the fall, Thomas decided to move the family once again. In an autobiography written in 1860, Abraham Lincoln mentioned his father's rationale

for moving as "partly on account of slavery, but chiefly on account of the difficulties of land titles in Kentucky."

Given modern ideas of political correctness and the myths that have grown around Abraham Lincoln, it is easy to assume that by "partly on account of slavery" he meant that his parents objected to slavery on moral grounds. Perhaps so, but it is also possible, the year being 1816, that the Lincolns' objections to slavery may have been economic or social. In the values of the time, slaves were valuable property and those who owned such property were held in a different economic and social class from those who did not. Also, slaves with certain marketable skills, such as cabinet making, were sometimes hired out by their owners, putting them in competition with craftsmen such as Thomas Lincoln. The Lincolns' attitude on the matter is one of those topics about which we shall never know more

This rear view of the Todd house suggests the grandeur of the place when the "garden which occupied the entire city block" is in bloom.

than we now do, but it seems probable that the objections to slavery were more economic than moral. A clue, however, is provided by the fact that the Hardin County Court records contain an order appointing Thomas Lincoln as a "padroler." In the early 19th century, every Kentucky county had patrolers (sometimes called "paddy rollers") whose duty was to prowl the county roads, arresting any fugitive slaves they encountered. It seems unlikely that a man with moral objections to slavery would accept such an appointment.

Some of the people in Hardin County at the time speculated that Lincoln's motive for moving was much more basic; that he decided to vacate the county to get away from Abraham Enloe. That's another one about which we will never know.

Whatever his motivation, history does record that Thomas Lincoln, having heard of rich and unoccupied land, to which one could obtain clear title from the federal government, in southwest part of Indiana, sold his interest in the Knob Creek farm. Liquidating his assets, he converted the cash to 400 gallons of whiskey – a pioneer currency – and loaded his woodworking tools and the spirits on a raft.

Launching the raft at the junction of Knob Creek and the Rolling Fork, he floated on the waters of the Rolling Fork to the Salt River and then down the Ohio to a point near Thompson's Ferry in Perry County, Indiana. On the way, the raft overturned once in the turbulent water, but he was able to retrieve his tools and most of the whiskey. Upon arrival, he left his goods with a local man and set out on foot in search of a home site. Walking northwest, within the first day, he had found a suitable location on Little Pigeon Creek about fifteen miles from the river near the present day town of Gentryville.

The site he selected was heavily forested and had a good spring nearby. Having made arrangements for his goods, he then walked back to Kentucky to escort his family to the new home site.

Perhaps with a sorrowful glance over the hill to where young Thomas lay buried, Thomas, Nancy, Sarah and seven-year old Abe walked away, their meager household goods loaded on two borrowed horses. Although Lincoln would always lay claim to being a Kentuckian, for the remainder of his life he would spend little time in his native state.

Looking north along Knob Creek to its intersection with the Rolling Fork of the Salt River.
This is the spot where Thomas Lincoln launched his raft for the move to Indiana.

INDIANA
1816
1830

*Relief Sculputre Panel depicting his Indiana years on the Visitor Center at the
Lincoln Boyhood National Memorial near Gentryville, Indiana.*

INDIANA
1816-1830

"It was a wild region, with many bears and other wild animals, still in the woods. There, I grew up."

– *Abraham Lincoln*

LINCOLN'S BOYHOOD HOME

Where it is: On Little Pigeon Creek near Lincoln City, Indiana

How Lincoln Got There: Walked most of the way, perhaps riding horseback some of the distance.

How You Can Get There: Take Exit 57 from Interstate 64. Follow US 231 South to Gentryville then IN 162 to Lincoln City.

In his 1860 autobiography, Abraham Lincoln spoke of the "unbroken forest" into which his family moved in the autumn of 1816. Driving across southern Indiana today, one is struck by how the landscape has changed. The flat land is disturbed only here and there by thickets of trees to serve as reminders of how the countryside looked two hundred years ago.

As the Lincolns left Kentucky with their meager possessions loaded onto two borrowed horses, clearly they took no furniture, depending instead on Thomas' cabinetmaking skills to supply their wants upon arrival at the new location. A few cooking implements, with perhaps some bedding and clothing made up the family's entire stock of worldly goods. There is no record of the exact date they left Kentucky or the route they followed, although many likely spots claim to have hosted the Lincolns on the trek. The distance "as the crow flies" is about eighty miles but their journey probably required traveling much farther considering the roads existent at the time.

Also, we do not know the date of arrival on the Little Pigeon Creek, in present day Spencer County, but Lincoln said it was "about the time the State came into the Union" (December 11, 1816.)

So, to build a shelter was an urgent necessity. Lincoln wrote (in the third person,) "...Abraham, though very young, was large for his age, and had an ax put in his hands at once." With his son's help, Thomas constructed what was called a "half faced" structure; a log lean-to-like affair closed on three side with the fourth – the south – side left open to the weather. Thus the fire could be build on the open side eliminating the need for a chimney. Such an arrangement might be fine for the spring and fall, but would not provide pleasant living conditions against the winds and snows of the Indiana winter. Nonetheless, the little family was to spend not only the winter of 1816, but the ensuing spring, summer and fall in this crude structure. Thomas Lincoln has been classed as a ne'er-do-well by many, but the fact that they remained in the camp for a year certainly does not imply idleness. During those seasons in the camp, in addition to hunting for meat, father and son chopped trees – using the logs for a cabin and to split into fence rails – pulled the stumps and cleared out rocks to create tillable land for the corn crop which would sustain them. That first year, they managed to raise six acres of corn.

One incident which occurred that first winter made such an impression on young Lincoln's mind that years later he wrote (again in the third person,) "At this place Abraham took an early start as a hunter, which was never much improved on afterward. A few days before the completion of his eighth year, in the absence of his father, a flock of wild turkeys approached the new log cabin, and Abraham, with a rifle-gun, standing inside, shot through a crack and killed one of them. He has never since pulled a

trigger on any larger game." This even though wild game abounded in the area, and hunting (and bragging about one's prowess) were favorite frontier pastimes. Abraham Lincoln usually had other things on his mind; if he wasn't working, he was telling tales at the store or reading.

As winter of 1817 approached, the Sparrow family, who had been neighbors back in Kentucky, arrived at the Little Pigeon Creek settlement. With them was Dennis Hanks, Nancy's nephew who had been adopted by the Sparrows. Dennis, nine years older than Lincoln, was Abe's cousin, friend and work-mate and, after Lincoln's death, by his own appointment, Dennis became Abe's confidant. Even though the cabin they had been building was only half completed, the Lincolns gave up the half-faced structure to the Sparrows and moved their possessions into the new structure.

Half completed or not, compared to the "camp," living in the new cabin must have been incredible luxury. Even though the door frame and window opening had no covering, the cabin did have four walls and a fireplace. Also, Thomas could construct some crude furniture of which there had been none in the camp. Young Abraham could climb to his roost in the loft on a ladder fashioned of wooden pegs driven into the wall. As a nine-year-old, he may have found that quite an adventure.

Over the years, the Indiana wilderness gradually gave way to civilization. A road from Corydon to Evansville came very near the Lincoln farm. A few years later when another

This stone is somewhere near Nancy Hanks Lincoln's actual grave site. The marker was "erected by a friend of her martyred son in 1879." It is strange that Abe Lincoln never placed a marker on his mother's grave. Note the pennies tossed by visitors.

A view of the "unbroken forest" near the Lincoln's "half-face" camp at Gentryville, IN.
Clearing a path for a wagon was a difficult chore that lingered in Abe's memory.

from Rockport to Bloomington created a crossroad, James Gentry claimed the land and when another man named Jones opened a store, the town of Gentryville began. The store would become a favorite hangout of Lincoln and it was here that he began his reputation as a story-teller.

In the fall of 1818, the "milksick" struck in Indiana. Today, we know that when cattle eat the white snakeroot, a plant common throughout the Ohio valley, they ingest a toxin which is poisonous to the animals and to humans who consume the milk or meat of infected cows. In 1818, however, all that was known about the disease was that a victim would develop a white coating on the tongue, usually along with loss of appetite and listlessness. Sometimes nausea and fever attended the disease and, if the victim went into a coma, the result was almost invariably death. Sometime in late August, both Tom and Betsy Sparrow were affected with the milksick and Nancy Lincoln went to attend them. Nonetheless, by September, both the Sparrows were dead. Shortly after they were buried in a clearing south of the cabin and camp, Nancy herself came down with the disease. As the nearest doctor was 30 miles away, her children may have tried to ease her pain and fever, but despite those efforts, on October 5, "Ma's sick" became "Ma's gone."

Tom Lincoln and Dennis Hanks made a rude coffin for her burial. Tradition has it that Abraham whittled the wooden pegs that held the planks together. However that may be, Nancy Hanks Lincoln was buried in the growing cemetery plot a few hundred yards from the cabin. Today, you can visit the cemetery and view the marker placed there, "by a friend of her martyred son" in 1879.

Although the exact location of her grave is unknown, she rests somewhere in the area under the shade of a huge locust tree and a shaggy-bark hickory. It is strange to note that even when he became a successful lawyer and President, Abraham Lincoln – one person who did know the actual burial location – never bothered to place a marker on his mother's grave. That fact, along with the fact that Lincoln seldom spoke of his mother and devoted all of two sentences to her in his autobiography, gives rise to much speculation about their relationship. But it is just that – speculation – as nobody knows what their relationship actually was or what kind of parent she was. So, Nancy Hanks Lincoln was dead at age 36, a time when a woman should be in her prime. Today, the ground around the stone marker is covered with

Lincoln pennies of various dates tossed there by visitors in some kind of a gesture to honor her or her son.

The Lincoln penny, incidentally, was first produced by the United States Mint in 1909 as a part of the Lincoln Centennial. The decision was controversial, as this coin was the first regular issue coin to ever bear a likeness of a President. Also, many citizens felt that one cent was too trivial to honor such a great man. Finally, there was a major outcry over the design of the coin; the objections concerned Victor David Brenner's, initials (VDB) on the reverse side of the coin at the bottom between the wheat stalks. The protest was so loud that the Secretary of the Treasury ordered the initials removed soon after the original issue. So, the 1909 "VDB." penny is rare, (about 28.5 million were struck, and then about 75 million without the VDB.) In 1918, the initials were restored,

The Lincoln penny was originally introduced in 1909 as a part of the Lincoln Centennial. The obverse side has remained basically unchanged.

The reverse side originally featured "V.B.D." the designer's initials. The design was changed from the "wheat ears" to the Lincoln Memorial configuration in 1959.

placed below Lincoln's shoulder, slightly to the left of center. The letters are so small that you will need a magnifier and a shiny new penny to see them. While you're looking at that shiny penny, note that the figure of Lincoln inside the Memorial is visible on the reverse.

In 1959, the "tails" side of the Lincoln penny was changed to depict the Lincoln Memorial. In 2009, which

As the designer's initials were initially too prominent, they were moved to the obverse side and made much less perceptible.

will mark Lincoln's bicentennial and the penny's 100th birthday, the reverse will be changed again, this time featuring four alternating scenes from Lincoln's life.

In his 1860 campaign autobiography, Abraham Lincoln left us the tantalizing tidbit from this same time frame that "in his tenth year he (Lincoln) was kicked by a horse and apparently killed for a time." Nothing else is known about that incident. Recent scientific scans of Lincoln's "life masks" have revealed a great asymmetry in his face which leads to some conjecture this accident may have caused the imbalance in his features. That asymmetry was noticed by Mount Rushmore sculptor Gutzon Borglum who described the left side of Lincoln's face as "primitive, immature and unfinished."

Frontier life was tough enough for a fully functioning family and nearly impossible without a wife and mother. Eleven year-old Sarah tried to assume the chores of cooking, cleaning, making and mending clothing and looking after her father and brother – and teenager Dennis Hanks, who had moved in since the Sparrows' deaths – but it soon became evident that the burden was too much for a young girl. Even so, the family suffered along for a little more than a year before Tom Lincoln, leaving Dennis, Abe and Sarah to fend for themselves, went back to Kentucky in search of a new wife.

In Elizabethtown, he found Sarah "Sally" Bush, the girl he had known before in Washington County. Sally was now

a widow, having married Daniel Johnson about the same time Tom had married Nancy Hanks. Daniel Johnson had subsequently been Hardin County jailer and had died of the "cold plague" in the summer of 1816. Sally had purchased a cabin just outside town and moved there with her three children. She was thirty-one years old; Thomas was 42.

The courtship was short. One report has Tom saying, "Well, *Miss* Johnson, I have no wife and you have no husband. I came a purpose to marry you: I knowed you from a gal and you knowed me from a boy. I have no time to lose, and if you're willin', let it be done straight off." Evidently she was willin'; Thomas Lincoln and Sally Bush

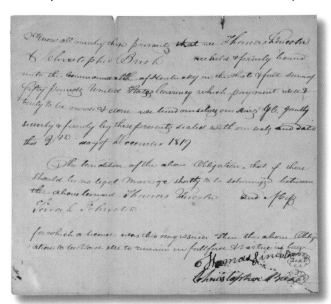

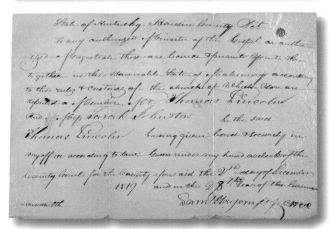

The marriage bond dated "the 2nd day of December 1819" bears the signatures of Thomas Lincoln and Christopher Bush and certifies that Thomas Lincoln intended to marry Sarah Bush Johnson. Courtesy of Hardin County, Kentucky County Clerk.

Johnson were married in Hardin County on December 2, 1819.

Sally had furniture, something sadly lacking in the Lincoln household. Dennis Hanks wrote of the "one fine bureau, one table, one set of chairs, one large clothes chest, cooking utensils, knives, forks, bedding and other articles" she brought to Indiana to furnish the cabin. So much baggage did she have that a four horse wagon was required to move her, her children and the "large supply of household goods." One can only imagine the wonder with which Abe and Sarah Lincoln viewed these riches being carried into their stark cabin. Of special delight to Abe was that Sally owned a few books, an interesting fact in view of her being illiterate.

Sally's first chore was to have her new husband provide the cabin with a floor, a door and a covering for the window, all of which were lacking. Given that she arrived in the middle of December, these items were surely needed.

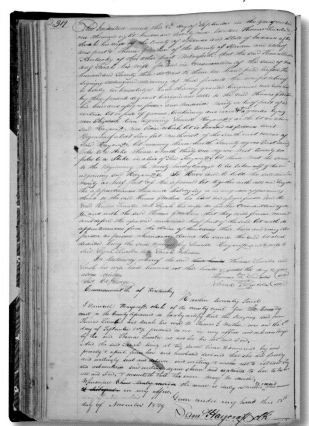

Thomas Lincoln and wife Sally returned to Elizabethtown, Kentucky to sell the property she owned. This deed, dated November 18, 1829, records the property transfer. Courtesy of Hardin County, Kentucky County Clerk.

Those who knew both families reported that "life among the Lincolns was a long ways below life among the Bushs." That fact evidently came home to Sally upon her arrival at the Lincoln homestead. She was "much surprised" at the difference between what she had been told about the place and the actual facts that she could observe. Nevertheless, she dove right into setting things right. She made no distinction between her own children – John, Sarah and Matilda – and her step children. Indeed, she washed the dirty Lincoln children and dressed the half naked boy and girl in clothing from the stores of her own children. Warm and clean, probably for the first time since the previous fall, it is little wonder that Abraham ever after referred to her as his "angel of a mother."

Many things about Abraham Lincoln's life may be unclear, but there is no doubt that Sally made a huge difference to him. "In fact," says Dennis Hanks, "in a few weeks, all had changed…. She was a woman of great energy, of remarkable good sense, very industrious and saving and also very neat and tidy in her person and manners and knew exactly how to manage children." With Tom and Sally, her three children, his two and Dennis Hanks, the eight people now living in the one-room cabin must have been really cozy. Indeed, Dennis Hanks, at age twenty, married Sally's daughter, Sarah Elizabeth, in 1821 when the bride had reached the mature age of fifteen.

There is some evidence that Thomas Lincoln was, in today's language, an abusive parent. Certainly, he had no interest in education either for himself or his children. Sally changed that, also. She wrote that she managed to influence her husband to allow the children to attend school. So, under her guidance, all the children went to school when it was in session during the winter and were encouraged to read and study on their own if they so desired. Abe attended three sessions of the same kind of "blab" school he had had in Kentucky, later estimating that "the aggregate of all his schooling did not amount to one year." Worth a note in passing is that Lincoln's twelve months of schooling took place over a period of nine years. Nonetheless, Sally encouraged her step-son to study when he was not working. According to her, he did it well: "Abe read diligently … He read every book he could lay his hands on; and when he came across a passage that struck him, he would write it down on boards if he had no paper,

and keep it there until he did get paper. Then he would rewrite it, look at it, repeat it. He had a copy-book, a kind of scrap book in which he put down all things and thus preserved them." One of the things he wrote in his copy book was a boyish poem:

Abraham Lincoln
His hand an pen
He will be good
But God knows when.

A glimpse into Lincoln's relationship with his father is provided by his step-sister, Matlida Johnson who indicated that Abe's propensity to mount a stump to speak "wherever he found the greatest number of people" greatly irritated Thomas. "When it was announced that Abe had taken the stump in the harvest field, there was an end of work. The hands flocked around him and listened to his curious speeches with infinite delight." Sally adds that, "while the sight of such a thing amused us all, my husband was compelled to break it up with a strong hand and poor Abe was many times dragged from the platform and hustled off to his work in no gentle manner."

Sometimes Abe wrote and "ciphered" on a fire shovel, a thinned board with one end narrowed for a handle. Useful as an implement for arranging coals under a skillet or oven, the broad face also served as a writing surface. When Abe had filled the entire writing space, he could scrape it off with a knife and begin again. While we have learned to take much of the American history we were taught in elementary school with a grain (if not a larger dose) of salt, evidently the image of Lincoln reading and writing by the flickering fire light is true. What's not in the grade school image is that Lincoln's devotion to reading was viewed by most of the community (and especially his father) as laziness, that his study may have been at the expense of his chores and he was, therefore, probably seen as something of a rebel.

Another of the Lincoln stories which appears to be true is of his borrowing Weems' *Life of Washington* from Josiah Crawford, a Pigeon Creek neighbor reputed to be pretty tight with a dollar. Legend has it that Abe stored the book overnight below an unchinked crack between two logs where it was damaged by rain water. Abe offered to pay for the book although he had no money. Consequently, he was required to pull fodder for Crawford for three days to pay for the book. Many years later, addressing the New

While excavating this boyhood home site in the 1930's, the remains of a cabin thought to be that built by Abe and his father in 1829 were discovered. These bronze logs and hearthstones mark the location.

Jersey Senate, President Lincoln told the senators that of all the passages in Weems' book, "…none fixed themselves on my imagination so deeply as the struggle here at Trenton." Evidently that book and Washington's crossing the Delaware River had a lasting impact on Abraham Lincoln.

There is no record to tell us when Lincoln reached his adult height of 6'4", but evidently he was that tall early in his teenage years. Strong and sinewy, he labored in the fields planting and plowing in season and clearing trees and splitting rails in off times. His strength and ability with an axe became legendary in the neighborhood. Friends relate that Lincoln could easily hold an axe by the handle at arms length and that when he put that tool to work, "it sounded like three men chopping." "My father taught me farm work," Lincoln once observed, "but he did not teach me to like it." Sensing at an early age that education was the key to escaping the farm work he disliked, Abe Lincoln applied his active mind to whatever studies he had available, even including wading through the multi-volume Indiana Revised Statutes – hard reading, to be sure.

> *"My father taught me farm work, but he did not teach me to like it."*
> – Lincoln

When the day's work was done, he'd head for Jones' store in Gentryville for a different kind of education. Such gathering places were the center of frontier social life, a place where yarns, gossip, news and just talk were swapped. Those who were there with Lincoln indicate that Abe participated in all those activities. Good natured and likable, he was good at talk and tales, earning a reputation for a good memory, a sharp wit and a wealth of stories. Like most humans, he had another side, too. Sometimes the dark and moody Lincoln would take precedence, the malady he would later call his "melancholy."

In late summer 1826, when Abe's sister Sarah married a local man named Aaron Grigsby, Abe may have seen an opportunity to break away. During the fall and winter of that year when farm work was on hold, Lincoln, easing out from his father's influence, was engaged in ferrying passengers from the mouth of Anderson Creek, on the Spencer County, Indiana side, to steamboats anchored in the middle of the Ohio River. River traffic was at its height, with travelers going upstream, migrants seeking new frontiers and loads of goods going downstream to market. His employer was James Taylor and his wage was six dollars per month and board. Incidentally, that wage is about the same as Lincoln earned when his father hired him out for farm work. A fact well known to all was that the steamboats headed for Louisville, Paducah, Cincinnati, Memphis and New Orleans would not wait, so Lincoln had a healthy business getting passengers to the boats on time. Although some records indicated that he sometimes helped out as a clerk at Jones' store, probably the first money Lincoln ever earned was by moving passengers and their luggage to the boats. On one memorable occasion, he had rowed two men to the middle of the river and hoisted their baggage on board, just as the steamer began to move away. When Lincoln yelled that they had not paid him, each man threw a half-dollar into Lincoln's boat. One dollar was probably the most money he had ever had at one time and that was earned in less than an hour! Many years later, he related the incident to his Cabinet in the White House; "I could scarcely believe my eyes as I picked up the money. Gentlemen, you may think it was a very little thing, and in these days it seems to me a trifle, but it was the most important incident in my life." On the banks of the Ohio River, at age 17, Abraham Lincoln widened his horizons, encountering people and ideas that he would never have found on the farm.

In the spring of 1827, Abe returned to his father's farm to help out with the plowing and planting, but now he had the river water in his blood and the farm surely seemed tame after the stint on the river. So, the fall of 1827 found him back on the river bank again, this time at Bate's Landing a mile or so below where he was the previous year. There, he built a flat boat hoping to secure a cargo to take down river.

Instead, he remained in the passenger business and this was to land him in a sort of trouble he never would have found on the farm. Abe had deposited some passengers in midstream and just returned to the Indiana shore when he saw a man hailing from the Kentucky side. Lincoln rowed over to discover that the man was John T. Dill, a Kentucky resident who operated a nearby ferry. As Lincoln stepped out of his boat, he was grabbed by Dill and his brother Lin, who had been hidden in the bushes. The Dills informed Lincoln that he was carrying passengers in violation of the

Kentucky statue and announced their intention to duck him in the river. After some discussion – probably heated and probably influenced by Lincoln's strength, the Dills' decided, instead, to take their grievance to court.

Thus agreed, the parties set out for the home of Squire Jeremiah Pate near Lewisport, just down the river . Lincoln probably thought he was indeed in trouble when the Squire greeted the Dills warmly. Pate was a former owner of the ferry, the Dills currently operated the ferry on Pate's land, they knew the Squire well and were, no doubt, confident that their arguments would prevail against the unlawful competitor. A warrant having already been sworn out by John T. Dill and all parties being present, the trial of the Commonwealth of Kentucky v. Abraham Lincoln promptly began.

The Dills proceeded to relate how they had witnessed, on several occasions, the defendant carrying passengers from the Indiana shore to steamboats in the river. Furthermore, they had seen the defendant accept pay for that service and so he was in violation of the law and their ferry rights.

The tall, gangly defendant stood to testify in his own behalf. Yes, he said, he had transferred passengers to the boats. No, he continued, he did not know there was any law against it and he did not feel that he had infringed on the ferry business as, in every case he could remember, the ferry was on the Kentucky side of the river when he picked up passengers and as is common knowledge, the boats will not wait. As the young man sat, surely, the sight of the strong, shoeless country boy dressed in buckskin and his obvious honesty impressed the Squire.

Both parties having been heard, the first issue was, as Lincoln had operated from the Indiana shore and never touched Kentucky's side, did the Hardin County court (it's in Hancock County now) have jurisdiction? Then, as now, the boundary of Kentucky is the high water mark on the north side of the river, so yes, Pate had jurisdiction and would decide the case.

Checking the Kentucky Revised Statutes, the Squire found that, "If any person whatsoever shall, for reward, set any person over any river or creek, whereupon public ferries are appointed, he or she so offending shall forfeit and pay five pounds current money for every such offense…." One can imagine the Squire adjusting his glasses and looking thoughtfully at Lincoln and the Dills as he pondered. Clearly, Lincoln had ferried passengers "for reward" but, as the judge saw it, "over" in the legal sense meant "across," not midstream. As no accusation was made and no testimony showed that the young boatman had set any person *across* the river, no offense had been committed and the warrant was, therefore, dismissed.

Legend has it that after the Dill brothers departed, no doubt discontented, Lincoln sat with Squire Pate on his porch while the Squire commented that ignorance of the law is no excuse, that every citizen should have a general knowledge of common law and every working man should know the details of laws pertaining to his particular profession. Much speculation has centered around this incident as setting Lincoln's mind on becoming a lawyer. No one knows just when Abraham made that decision, but at least a decade was to pass before he began to "read law" in earnest. However, it is a fact that soon after the Dill episode was when he undertook the reading of the Indiana Revised Statutes made available by the local constable, David Turnham.

In January 1828, tragedy came once again to Abraham Lincoln when his sister, Sarah Grigsby, died in childbirth. She is buried – her stillborn child in her arms – beside her husband in the Little Pigeon Baptist Church yard. Abe had now buried his mother and his sister in the Indiana soil.

But, life goes on. In April 1828, the richest man in the community, James Gentry, hired Lincoln to accompany his son, Allen, down the Mississippi on a flatboat with a "cargo-load" of produce, New Orleans being the best market. Although, to quote Lincoln, he was "merely a hired hand," the fact that Gentry chose him speaks well for the nineteen-year-old's character. Gentry obviously thought him trustworthy and capable of handling whatever difficulties and trouble might be encountered on the 1200 mile trip.

Lincoln and the young Gentry traveled down to the

> *"I could scarcely believe my eyes as I picked up the money. Gentlemen, you may think it was a very little thing, and in these days it seems to me a trifle, but it was the most important incident in my life."*
> – Lincoln

Ohio River at Rockport, Indiana to begin the trip. Each young man was to be paid eight dollars per month and return passage on a steamboat for his labors. We can well imagine the conversation between the two young men off on an adventure – tales of what they'd see and do on arrival, how'd they'd spend the money they were earning and how home folks would be impressed when they related those encounters upon their return to Little Pigeon Creek.

Evidently the journey was placid enough floating down the Ohio into the Mississippi and then down past the Tennessee and Arkansas shores until one evening when they were docked for the night at a plantation just above their destination. Lincoln himself tells us: "… one night (we) were attacked by seven negroes with intent to kill and rob (us.) (We) were hurt some in the melee but managed in driving the negroes from the boat…." Abe did not relate that the "driving" was done by himself with a club and that he received a wound over his left eye that left a scar. Fearing that the marauders would return, the two boys returned to the boat to "cut cable." Swinging into the current they drifted until daylight relieved their fears. It is also possible that this incident may have been a factor in the left side of his face being smaller than the right –

which was therefore, according to period photographers, his "good" – side

New Orleans in all its early nineteenth century splendor must have been a sight for two Indiana country boys to behold. Its narrow streets, crowded wharfs, cathedrals, warehouses, and pastel stucco houses with iron railings were something surely not to be found on Little Pigeon Creek. Likewise, the markets' offerings of fresh seafood, tropical fruit and southern grain and meats were as unknown to the impressionable visitors as were the accents and languages and dress of the foreign people they encountered. Evidently Lincoln did indeed see his first slave market at this time. Much has been written about the impression the selling of human beings made on Lincoln, but neither he, nor anyone else who may have known, made any mention of it.

Boarding one of the luxurious steamboats of the era, the youths made their way back to Indiana. Steam travel being at its height, the boats were populated by all manner of passengers, prostitutes and riverboat gamblers. With the ports, such as the infamous Natchez Under the Hill, being dens of iniquity, the return trip must have been an education in itself for two Indiana backwoods boys. They arrived in June with twenty-four dollars each in

From this site on the Ohio at Rockport, IN, Abe and Allen Gentry departed for New Orleans in 1828.

This plaque at Rockport marks the riverfront location. The boys faced a challenging trip of some 1000 miles down the Ohio River and then the Mississippi.

their pockets and a wealth of stories to share (and perhaps some not to be shared) with the home folks. Lincoln was evidently unchanged by the trip, still a likeable, physically strong and strong willed young man seeking to further his education so as to remove himself from the physical labor he disliked. Nonetheless, being under twenty-one years of age, he dutifully went back to his father's farm work.

By the next fall, Thomas Lincoln had his son and sons-in-law at work building a new cabin. It is unclear whether this cabin was ever finished, as by the early spring of 1830, the elder Lincoln once again had the urge to move. When work was underway on Indiana's Nancy Hanks Lincoln Memorial Park in the mid-1930's, the remains of a cabin purported to be the 1829 Lincoln cabin were unearthed a few hundred yards north of Nancy's grave site. Today, the site is marked by bronze sill logs and hearth stones on "the traditional site of a log cabin home built by Thomas Lincoln and his son, Abraham." Visiting there, you may, if you like, take in the "living historical farm," and walk the one-mile "trail of twelve stones," a pleasant stroll through the Indiana woods interrupted here and there by displays of stones from sites important to Abraham Lincoln's life, such as the Mary Todd Lincoln house in Lexington, KY and the original "President's Mansion" in Washington, DC.

Late in 1829 or early 1830, Thomas and Sally Lincoln went back to Kentucky, to Elizabethtown to sell the lot she had inherited upon the death of her first husband. The county clerk certified that he examined Mrs. Lincoln privately and that she did "freely and willingly" agree to the sale.

Thomas Lincoln had simply "squatted" on government land for most of the time he had been in Indiana, but finally did pay $2.00 per acre for 80 acres. Aside from a new wife, he was no better off after 14 years, and having heard of rich farm land – free of the "milksick" – over in Illinois, he determined to go there. Early in 1830, he agreed to sell the Indiana farm for $125 – less than he'd paid – and prepared to leave. Combined with the money from the Elizabethtown property, he had enough to buy three teams of oxen to pull the wagons.

Although by the time they were ready to go, Abraham would be twenty-one years of age and legally free to do as he pleased, he chose to remain with his family until the move was accomplished. Accordingly, he helped produce the lumber required to build the wagons to haul the household goods and family members on the journey. And a big family it was: Dennis and Sarah Hanks with their four children, Sally's other daughter, Matilda with her husband and child, the three Lincolns and Sally's son John comprised the company.

On Monday morning March 1, 1830, amid the creaking of wooden-spoked wheels and the shouts of the drivers, Abraham being one, the Lincolns turned their backs to the rising sun and departed the land where they had spent more than a decade – the same land where Nancy and Sarah lay buried. Once again they would seek a better life, this time on the black prairie soil of Illinois.

On an 1844 Whig campaign tour of Indiana for the benefit of his political idol, Henry Clay, Lincoln visited his mother's grave. "That part of the county ..." he wrote, "is as unpoetical as any spot on earth; but still, seeing it ... Aroused in me feelings which were certainly poetry." Leaving us a rare insight into his emotions, Abraham Lincoln wrote down some of those poetic feelings:

My childhood's home I see again,
And sadden with the view;
And still, as memory crowds my brain,
There's pleasure in it too.

Relief Sculputre Panel depicting his Illinois years on the Visitor Center at the Lincoln Boyhood National Memorial near Gentryville, Indiana.

ILLINOIS
1830 - 1861

To this place and the kindness of these people, I owe everything.

– *Abraham Lincoln*

LINCOLN'S FIRST ILLINOIS HOME
1830-1831

Where It is: Near Decatur, Illinois about halfway between Springfield and Champaign

How Lincoln got there: Drove an ox cart from Indiana

How you get there: Travel on Interstate 72 in Central Illinois

Illinois is indeed the "Land of Lincoln." Not only did he live in Illinois for the majority of his life, but as a circuit-riding attorney, he visited hundreds of venues in Illinois. Unfortunately for us, at many of those sites today, there is nothing more than a historical marker. At the remaining venues, however, there is plenty to see and experience.

After a journey of some two weeks, sometime within the month of March 1830, the Lincoln party arrived at a site already selected by one of Abe's mother's relatives, John Hanks. The location was in Macon County "on the north side of the Sangamon River, at the junction of the timberland and prairie, about ten miles westerly from Decatur," according to Lincoln. This is one of the venues where there is little for us to see now.

By the time the Lincoln party arrived, John Hanks had already felled numerous trees for a cabin. Tom, Abe, Dennis Hanks and Sally's son John Johnson set right into building the cabin, splitting fence rails, fencing and breaking the ground and planting a corn crop. That first year, they raised ten acres of corn. Concerning the fence rails, in 1860, Lincoln said that "these are, or are supposed to be, the rails about which so much is being said just now, though these are far from being the first or only rails ever made by Abraham." So, again, in the Lincoln legend, we see that although "The Rail Splitter" was a campaign slogan, it happened to be true.

In fact, how that slogan originated is an interesting tale. In May 1860, in conjunction with the Illinois Republican Convention being held in Decatur, local lawyer Richard Oglesby happened to be talking to John Hanks concerning Lincoln's possible nomination for President. When John mentioned the fence-building activities of the spring of 1830, Oglesby asked if Hanks thought any of that fence might still be there. Hanks said that although he had not been to the site in more than ten years, there were still plenty of rails when he was last there. Upon arrival at the old Lincoln cabin site, the two men found a fence made of black walnut and honey locust rails. Hanks announced that these were indeed the rails he and Lincoln had made thirty years before. Hauling two of the fence rails back to Decatur, Oglesby then exhibited them at the convention with a banner attached declaring Abraham Lincoln as "The Rail Candidate for President 1860."

That incident supplied not only the campaign slogan – from that day forward, Lincoln was "The Rail Splitter" – but it also supplied John Hanks with a steady income: He sold those two rails for five dollars each and then went back the next day for an entire wagon load of rails which he sold for $1 each. After Lincoln became famous and certainly after his death, many times the number of rails split by Hanks and Lincoln (those two said it was about 3000) were sold throughout the United States.

In the fall of 1830, everyone at the Lincoln cabin site

came down with "ague and fever." So discouraged where they that the decision was made to return to Indiana the following spring. A long hard winter lay between them and the departure, however. The winter of 1830-31 became the "winter of the deep snow" in Illinois. Come spring, Thomas Lincoln did depart, but now twenty-one year-old, and hence free agent, Abraham did not go with him. Tom eventually settled in Coles County Illinois and would be a very small part of his son's life thereafter.

In late winter, Abraham, John Hanks and John Johnson, remaining in Macon County, agreed with a glib merchant named Dennis Offutt to take a flatboat of Offutt's goods from Beardstown to New Orleans. For that purpose, they were to meet Offutt in Springfield as soon as the weather cleared. The snow did melt about the first of March, but left the roads in such a muddy condition as to be impassable. So, the trio of adventurers bought a canoe and paddled down the Sangamon. Offutt was indeed at Beardstown – drunk in a tavern – but he

had not managed to get a boat at Beardstown, which is about 35 miles further west on the Illinois River. That probably came as no surprise to Lincoln – Offutt was a wheeler-dealer with a reputation for being mostly talk. Nevertheless, Lincoln, Hanks, and Johnson agreed to build a boat and take Offutt's goods down river on it for $12 per month each.

With himself as "chief cook and bottle washer," Lincoln and the others went a little up river from Springfield. On government land, they felled trees and constructed a crude flatboat. After the cargo was loaded, they set off down the Sangamon, bound for the Illinois, then the Ohio, and then the Mississippi headed for New Orleans. But, before they managed any of that, the boat lodged on a mill dam at New Salem. The boat was firmly stuck with the bow pointed skyward and the stern under water. While the local residents enjoyed the unexpected entertainment, shouting advice and catcalls, Lincoln went ashore to borrow an auger from the local cooper's. He then used the implement

A reproduction of Rutledge Mill is on the exact site of the original on the Sangamon River. Note the dam constructed to funnel water through the mill. When the river channel, now marked by the trees visible through the porch, shifted, New Salem was no longer a viable community.

One original New Salem building, the cooper's shop, still exists.

to bore a hole in the bow bottom and redistributed the cargo, thereby creating a better balance. Moving the goods toward the bow caused the boat to rock forward, which, in turn, caused the water in the stern to run toward the bow where it drained out the hole drilled for the purpose. Legend has it that by this means, Lincoln managed to get the boat unstuck, even though no one seems to have actually witnessed the event. At any rate, somehow, he got the flatboat over the dam.

The story goes that with the dam crossed, Lincoln quickly plugged the hole and they were on their way to New Orleans. The New Salem residents who had witnessed the feat – however it was done – were much impressed with the young man's ingenuity.

As, evidently was Denton Offutt, who, according to Lincoln, "conceived a liking" for him. The two agreed that upon Lincoln's return from the river trip, he would "act as clerk in charge of a store and mill at New Salem, then in Sangamon County, now in Menard." Lincoln stayed a

while to take in the sights of New Orleans, then worked his way home, firing the boiler on a steamboat.

John Hanks reported that Abe saw the slave markets in New Orleans on this trip and that Lincoln's "heart bled" and that Lincoln's attitude toward slavery was there formed. However, in his 1860 autobiography, Lincoln states that John Hanks started the trip, but "....having a family and being likely to be detained from home longer than at first expected, had turned back from St. Louis." Evidently, then, John Hanks was one of the many who tried to enlarge his role in Lincoln's life.

Back in Illinois, after a few days at his father's farm, Abe shook hands with Thomas and bade him an easy farewell. Saying goodbye to Sally was probably not as easy as he wrapped his long arms around her and tried to find some way to say "thank you" for all her kindness. With leave-takings accomplished, in July 1831, twenty-one year-old Abraham Lincoln "stopped indefinitely and for the first time, as it were, by himself at New Salem."

LINCOLN'S NEW SALEM

1831-1837

Where It Is: About 10 miles north-west of Springfield near Petersburg, IL.

How Lincoln Got There: Probably walked up from the Ohio River, perhaps from St. Louis

How You can get there: Take Interstate 55 or 72 to Springfield, then IL 97 to New Salem

Part I

When Abraham Lincoln returned from his New Orleans trip in July 1831 as "a piece of floating driftwood," New Salem was a thriving river community of perhaps twenty log cabins (several of which had two rooms) and perhaps 100 residents, boasting, in addition to the mill and cooper's shop, a church, stores, a blacksmith, a doctor, a tavern, and a tannery. As there were no railroads and virtually no roads in Illinois, the rivers and streams presented the major means of travel. Hence this spot on the Sangamon River was on the northern edge of the Illinois frontier. The town was founded a couple of years before Lincoln's arrival when James Rutledge had constructed a dam (the very one on which Lincoln's boat had lodged back in the spring) to provide for a water-powered grist and lumber mill.

At loose ends waiting for Offutt's goods to arrive, Lincoln lounged about the village with little to do, other, maybe, than wondering if Offutt would indeed make good on his promise to open a store. Perhaps he picked up a few odd jobs here and there, but being the town loafer probably did not irritate him much; he surely did not miss the arduous farm work. With some money in his pocket from the New Orleans trip, sitting around telling tales and swapping stories with

Rutledge Mill, which functioned as a sawmill as well as a grist mill, is a marvel of nineteenth century engineering. These sprockets drive the sawmill track.

This long view show the track which utilized water power to move logs through the saw blade.

the New Salem folks was probably much to his liking. He boarded with the Rutledge family who owned the mill and had a good-looking daughter named Ann. James Rutledge also happened to be the organizer of the New Salem Debating Society.

A month or so after Lincoln's arrival, a local election was held in New Salem. Abe had evidently made an impression of the residents as he was appointed as clerk of the election board. In slack times around the polling places, Lincoln regaled those in attendance with his stories and became fast friends with a local teacher named Mentor Graham, who was a member of the election board. Graham who, incidentally, says he was in Hardin County, Kentucky when Abe was a boy and often saw him, but never spoke, later remembered the "facility, fairness and honesty which characterized the new clerk's work."

A few days later, Lincoln was hired to pilot a boat to Beardstown. By the time he walked back to New Salem, Offutt's goods had arrived, so his job as store clerk began. Before long, Offutt, always on the lookout for

an opportunity, had leased the Rutledge mill and placed Lincoln in charge of that enterprise also, with William Green as his aide. The two men slept together in the back room of the store, on a bed so narrow that "when one of us turned over, the other was obliged to do likewise." Lincoln and Green became lifelong friends.

An episode made famous by Hollywood movies is the encounter between Abe Lincoln and Jack Armstrong. Armstrong, a resident of nearby Clary's Grove, "a hardy, strong, well-developed specimen of physical manhood," was considered by one and all the local "king of the hill." Offutt's continual bragging on Lincoln's strength, talent, and abilities brought on a heated discussion in the store over Lincoln's ability to deal with Armstrong. Although Lincoln refused to wrestle, eventually so much talk was generated and so much money bet on the outcome that a match was unavoidable. With the entire town in attendance, there are as many descriptions of the outcome as witnesses, but the consensus is that neither could best the other in the friendly contest and that they eventually

agreed to call the match a draw, shook hands and became friends. That friendship was to prove of benefit to both parties.

Most of New Salem's residents were from the South – the frontier was moving north and west, so many were born in Kentucky, Virginia or Tennessee – and many were well educated. Lincoln was able to borrow books to

Reproduction of Offutt's Store where Lincoln first served as a clerk.

indulge his love of reading and, with Mentor Graham's help, (and possibly insistence) he began to study grammar and math. By the fall of 1831, Lincoln had become active in the debating society and, while he demonstrated wit and intelligence, his lack of education was exposed. Graham advised the young man that if he intended to speak in public, he should learn proper grammar.

Evidently Lincoln did plan on doing some public speaking. On March 15, 1832 he placed an announcement in the *Sanagmo Journal* which began "Fellow Citizens: Having become a candidate for the honorable office of one of your representatives in the next General Assembly of this state …it becomes my duty to make known to you – the people whom I propose to represent – my sentiments with regard to local affairs." In the text of the article, he addressed the problems, as he saw them, then facing the New Salem district, those being, primarily, communications and transportation issues, but also interest rates and education. This announcement includes a formal alignment with the principles of Henry Clay's

The store offered leather goods, whiskey, glassware and other products which could not be produced on the farm; nearly everything except food.

Whig Party, which sponsored what we call "infrastructure" today. Being a Whig was an interesting – and courageous – choice in a country which was almost universally devoted to President Andrew Jackson's Democratic Party. The announcement concludes, in what would become typical Lincoln rhetoric, "Every man is said to have his peculiar ambition. Whether it be true or not, I can say that I, for one, have no other so great as that of being truly esteemed of my fellow men, by rendering myself worthy of their esteem…." The announcement is thoughtfully and skillfully written, especially in view of the age and education of its author. No doubt, he was encouraged by his friends to try for the representative post, but Lincoln himself reports that "Offutt's business was failing – had almost failed" by this time, so perhaps needing some form of employment also played a part in his decision to run for office.

In April 1832, before Lincoln had time to make any campaign speeches, Sauk and Fox Indian chief Black Hawk broke his treaty with the United States government by re-crossing the Mississippi River, with 500 well-mounted and well-armed warriors, into the Illinois country he had agreed to vacate. Illinois Governor Reynolds called for volunteers from the state militia to repel the "invasion." Abraham Lincoln was among the first to respond, volunteering for 30 days service. On April 21, he was sworn into a company consisting mostly of New Salem men, including the "king of the hill," Jack Armstrong. As a Presidential candidate, Lincoln said in his autobiography that his being elected Captain of the company came as a complete surprise and that he, "has not since had any success in life which gave him so much satisfaction." Abraham Lincoln appears to have always been proud of his military service despite the fact that he often downplayed it and one of his first orders to the company earned him the response "Go to hell" from the troops. He met many men who would later play a part in his career, one of whom was Lieutenant Robert Anderson, the man who would be in command of besieged Fort Sumter in 1861.

Lincoln's term of service – he re-enlisted for another 30 days two additional times – was undistinguished and bloodless, except for his "bloody struggles with the mosquitoes," and perhaps cost him the election as he was defeated in the fall. Another part of the Lincoln myth was generated during his time as Captain, however, and it is, apparently, also true. He knew, of course, nothing of military tactics and maneuvers. As his company marched in formation up to a narrow gate, Lincoln could not devise a command to get them through. Calling a halt, he ordered the men dismissed, to reform on the other side of the gate in five minutes. Evidently, the men performed the maneuver as ordered. Even if his absence from the campaign cost him his first run for office, the time in the military was well spent as he made several friends who would be valuable in the years to come.

The discharged warrior returned to New Salem with $125 pay and an Iowa land grant for his service. A mere ten days remained before the election day in which he was a candidate, leaving only enough time to make a few speeches. Most of his speaking was in New Salem, but he also appeared on one occasion in Springfield where he was unknown except to a few former comrades-in-arms. Not surprisingly, Lincoln was defeated despite earning a 277-3 vote in the New Salem district. This political defeat in the beginning of his career was not a total loss, however. He clearly earned the respect of his fellow townsmen, met several men who would prove to be valuable friends, gained experience in thinking on his feet and increased his confidence is his abilities.

Part II

In the fall of 1832, with his military service ended, Offutt's store out of business and, although encouraged for a political future, defeated in his bid for public service, Abraham Lincoln needed a job.

At the reconstructed New Salem village of today, the story of Rowan Herndon having accidentally shot his wife is legendary. Whatever the circumstances, store-keeper Herndon desired to leave the area and so sold his half interest in a store to Abe. Lincoln signed a note for the purchase and thus became a partner of William Berry, who had been in Lincoln's company in the war and owned the other half of the business. Before the Lincoln-Berry enterprise was fairly well begun, the partners purchased an additional stock of goods from James Rutledge who had acquired the merchandise in payment of a debt. This store would have offered goods which most folks could

The Lincoln-Berry enterprise led to Mr. Lincoln's "National Debt."

not produce locally – coffee and tea, whiskey, flour, leather goods, salt, sugar, tools, cooking implements and almost anything except food. As if Lincoln and Berry didn't have enough goods and debt, a short while later, the infamous Clary's Grove boys, in a drunken fracas, wrecked merchant Reuben Radford's store. Disgusted, Radford remarked that he'd sell out to the first man who would make him an offer. As fate would have it, William Green, Lincoln's assistant in the Offutt ventures happened along at that moment. Hearing Radford's lament, Green said, "Sell out to me." Asked to make an offer, Green surveyed the wreckage and offered $400 which Radford readily accepted. In the accepted practice of the day, Green paid $23 in cash and signed notes for the balance. Usually, one paid a debt by signing over notes he held from someone else. One gets the impression that every man in New Salem held at least one note from some other resident.

Before long, Lincoln had the news of his old friend Green being a new competitor. Viewing the remains of the Clary's Grove boys' work, Abe suggested that he and Green take an inventory. Obviously not understanding the term, but evidently suspecting it meant the kind of celebration that caused the damage in the first place, Green responded, "Abe, I don't believe this store can stand another one just at this time." The misunderstanding straightened out, they conducted an inventory, determining the goods to be worth some $900. Berry and Lincoln bought the stock from Green, paying $265 in cash, assuming the notes Green had given Radford and throwing Berry's horse and saddle into the deal.

Berry and Lincoln moved the new stock into their building and probably congratulated themselves on having bought out the competition. But any riches they envisioned were not to be. A large portion of the stock consisted of whiskey of which Mr. Berry was overly fond. Apparently without his partner's knowledge, Berry applied for a liquor license – the right to sell liquor by the drink – and soon managed to have the business failing. In view of that development and as Lincoln did not drink and did not approve of Berry's imbibery, he sold his interest in the store to Berry, obtaining Berry's note for the debt. Within a short time after becoming sole owner, Berry had managed to "drink up the profits" and so sold out to the Trent brothers, who paid, of course, by signing notes. Such a "house of credit" is bound to collapse and so it did when the Trents skipped town. Berry then assumed operation of the store again and was involved in it until his death. From a debt standpoint, Berry's death left Lincoln sort of like the one without a seat in a game of musical chairs as he was now responsible for all the various notes. And, once again, he had no means of earning a living.

He did have, however, health, intelligence, strength, the respect and affection of the town folks and, perhaps most importantly to him, the affection of Miss Ann Rutledge.

One of today's romance novelists could not produce a better story than the Lincoln/Rutledge affair. Consider the plot: "Prettiest girl in town is engaged to rich, handsome bachelor. Bachelor abandons damsel who only then sees the kindness and sincerity of lowly backwoods suitor. Pretty girl and backwoodsman agree to marry, but romance is foiled by her untimely death." Well, that's the way it actually happened.

There seems to be a great deal of controversy concerning the relationship between Ann and Abe, but most of that is apparently because Lincoln's last law partner and biographer, Billy Herndon, mishandled the story. Soon after Lincoln's death Herndon began collecting data – mostly through interviews – about his slain partner. He learned, from numerous sources, about the Lincoln-Rutledge affair. Herndon came to believe with his whole heart that Ann Rutledge was the root case of Lincoln's well-known melancholy.

Then, in 1866, Herndon committed the unpardonable

sin of going on a lecture tour, revealing the facts he had learned for his own profit, much to the dismay of Lincoln's wife and son, who, of course, knew nothing of Miss Rutledge. Furthermore, the Lincolns did not believe Herndon's story and did not want to believe it. Additionally, Herndon embellished the facts to make his show more sensational. Therefore, later historians – without knowing what Herndon knew – have suggested that Herndon gave the lecture and exaggerated the relationship purely out of his dislike for Mary Todd Lincoln. When Herndon's papers were acquired by the Library of Congress in 1941, the world learned that the information Herndon collected overwhelmingly indicates that Ann Rutledge and Abe Lincoln were much in love and, no doubt, would have married had she not died.

All agree that Ann was pretty, quick-witted, gentle and full of kindness. Most who knew her say that she was beloved and respected by everyone in New Salem. So it is not surprising that all the young men were after her, including postmaster Samuel Hill, Lincoln's store partner William Berry, a young man named John McNeil, and Abe Lincoln.

Miss Rutledge was born in Kentucky on January 7, 1813, so would have been 20 years old in 1833 when Lincoln returned from the Black Hawk War. She was engaged to marry McNeil at that time, having rejected Hill and Berry. All reporters, including McNeil himself, agree that he had to confess that he was living in New Salem under an assumed name – his name was actually John McNamar – and that he went to New York to help his parents with some difficulty. McNamar thus dismisses himself from the discussion by saying then, that he knew nothing of any relationship between Ann and Abe, as he was absent. If he was engaged to Ann, he failed to mention that fact in his correspondence with Herndon. Everybody else, however, agrees that they were engaged and that, in McNamar's absence, she and Lincoln came to terms and became engaged. Miss Rutledge refused to marry Lincoln, however, until she had the opportunity to discuss the situation with McNamar and obtain an honorable release from her promise to him. Some circumstance delayed McNamar's return to Illinois and Ann Rutledge contracted brain fever and died on August 25, 1835 before she had any opportunity to speak with him and thus become free.

One point on which there is no controversy is that Abraham Lincoln took Ann's death very hard. Everyone who knew Lincoln at the time said that while he had been quite sprightly and full of jokes and pranks before, he went into deep melancholy following her death. So depressed was he that friends had to remove razors and knives from his presence for fear of his committing suicide. Having the opportunity to observe Lincoln's sadness many years later, Herndon assumed that Ann Rutledge was still on his mind. Herndon says that with reference to Ann's grave, his partner told him, "My heart is buried there."

Just to add a little more twist to the story, Ann Rutledge was originally buried on property owned by John McNamar. That gentleman said that he bought the property in 1831 – before he went to New York and before her death – and that he placed the marker on her grave. If he indeed owned the property at the time, he did not say why – or how – she came to be buried there. In 1890, a body purported to be Ann Rutledge's was disinterred and moved to Oakland Cemetery in Petersburg, IL where you may visit today.

The store debacle left Lincoln with what he called his "personal national debt." Unlike many of the time who would just skip to a new town to avoid paying a debt, Lincoln was determined to pay it all off and to stay among the friends he'd made, so he stuck to New Salem,

Plenty of other things were going on in Lincoln's life at this time as well. New Salem was a tight knit community where politics may have been a major source of entertainment, but not to the extent that the men did not respect each other's views. Unlike the places Lincoln had lived before, New Salem was a booming river town which attracted many different kinds of people, all with different interests: cock fights, horse races, horse shoe tournaments, debates, quilting bees, wrestling matches, shooting matches, militia training, hunting and dances were all a part of life in 1830's New Salem. Abraham Lincoln participated in many of these activities and was, by consensus, the strongest man in town.

In consideration of the boom, plenty of work was available, mostly of the physical labor variety. But Lincoln wanted to earn a living using his brains instead of his muscles. He still read everything he could lay hands on, but also studied grammar, math and finally, surveying. On

After the river shifted, New Salem disappeared to be reconstructed in the 1930's. One of the reproductions looks much like the building where Lincoln served as Post Master.

May 7, 1833 Abraham Lincoln was appointed postmaster of New Salem by no less that the ultimate Democrat, President Andrew Jackson. Lincoln laughed that off by remarking that the office "was too insignificant to make his politics an objection." One story has it that the local women, being disgruntled by the illicit behavior of Samuel Hill, the previous postmaster, petitioned the President to make the appointment, but a more likely possibility is that a local Democrat intervened on Lincoln's behalf. Like all such appointees, he was required to post a $500 bond – two local Democrats loaned him the money. However he got the appointment, he retained the office for three years until the New Salem office was eliminated by the government.

That job provided little income. The postmaster's pay depended on the office revenue and, while there are no actual records for the New Salem office, others on the same route indicate that Lincoln probably made $25-$30 per year. More importantly, the job gave him the opportunity to become acquainted with everybody in the area and to read every newspaper that came through the office. In those days, patrons had to come to the post office to pick up mail as home delivery was unknown. But if Lincoln knew that someone was particularly anxious over a letter, when it arrived, he'd close the office (usually leaving the door unlocked so folks could pick up mail) to take it to the recipient's home. If he had an appointment somewhere in the country, he'd pack the mail for everybody in the vicinity in his hat – carrying papers in his hat became a life-long habit – and distribute it along the way. Also, as postmaster, he was exempt from militia service and jury duty, was free to study his borrowed surveying texts and, as the job was not confining, seek other sources of income. He also took full advantage of the franking privilege to write letters of editorial to the *Sangamo Journal*.

Lincoln's study paid off in the fall of 1833 when he was appointed deputy surveyor of Sangamon County. Again, this being a county office, politics were probably involved and Lincoln's appointment was likely aided by some Democrat. Knowing the political affiliations of John Calhoun, who was the county surveyor and a staunch Democrat, Lincoln hesitated, agreeing to accept the position only after being assured that no politics were involved in the work. Once again, this speaks well of Lincoln's standing in the community. By January of 1834, having obtained a horse, a surveyor's compass and chain, Lincoln was ready to begin work as a surveyor.

As the country was filling rapidly with settlers, there were farms to be surveyed, towns to be laid out and roads to be opened; surveying was an important job. At last Lincoln had a semi-reliable source of income to live comfortably and to help him pay off his "national debt." Even today, you can see the results on Lincoln's work as a surveyor in several roads and the town of Petersburg, near New Salem.

Not many of Lincoln's stories have survived, perhaps because many were considered "vulgar" by nineteenth century standards, but here's one he supposedly told on himself from his surveying days. It seems that being boarded in a private home one night, Lincoln was put to bed in the same room with two girls, the head of his bed being next to the foot of the girls' bed. In the night, he began tickling one of the girl's feet with his fingers. As she seemed to enjoy this as much as he did, he then tickled at little higher up; and as he would tickle higher, the girl would slide down lower. The higher he tickled, the lower she slid down in the bed. "Mr. Lincoln would tell the story with evident enjoyment," said one who heard it, but, "he never told how the thing ended."

In his capacity as postmaster and also as surveyor, Lincoln had the opportunity to meet and know almost everybody in the countryside. He liked and was liked by them all, his judgment was always respected – he frequently was called upon to arbitrate disputes on points of literature, mathematics and folk lore – he was willing to lend his strength to work projects and his good humor and storytelling were legendary. All things considered, Abe Lincoln exhibited all the ingredients for a successful politician.

Part III

On April 19, 1834, Abraham Lincoln's name appeared in the *Sangamo Journal* announcing his candidacy for the state legislature. No doubt encouraged by his many friends and buoyed by his showing in the previous bid for public office despite the adverse circumstances, he once again avowed his allegiance to Henry Clay's Whig party. Abner Ellis, A New Salem friend, reports accompanying Lincoln to make a speech at Island Grove where the Jackson men (Democrats) tried to make sport of the gangly Whig. "He told the boys several stories which drew them after him. I remember them, but modesty and my veneration for his memory forbids me to relate." According to Ellis, Lincoln said:

"Gentlemen and fellow citizens; I presume you all know who I am. I am humble Abraham Lincoln and I have been solicited by many friends to become a candidate for the legislature. My politics are short and sweet like the old woman's dance. I am in favor of a national bank. I am in favor of the internal improvement system and a high protective tariff. Those are my sentiments and political principles. If elected, I shall be thankful and if not, it will all be the same."

Election day, as specified by the Illinois Constitution as the first Monday in August in even number years, fell on August 4, 1834. Among thirteen candidates, the four highest vote-getters would be elected to represent the district in the Eighth Illinois Legislature. Lincoln finished first in the voting, six votes ahead of the second place man. The man in fourth place was one of Lincoln's Black Hawk War friends, John T. Stuart. Stuart, like Lincoln, was a Kentuckian (as a matter of fact, the T. in his name was for Todd, he was Mary Todd's cousin) and, although a few years older, a political rookie. Their friendship would provide future benefits to

FARMINGTON

Historic residence completed 1816 for John and Lucy (Fry) Speed. The Jefferson-inspired plan by Paul Skidmore includes octagonal rooms, rare in 19th c. Kentucky. As many as 64 African Americans enslaved at Farmington worked the 550-acre hemp plantation. Abraham Lincoln spent three weeks here in 1841 as guest of the family of his closest friend, Joshua Speed.

2007   KENTUCKY HISTORICAL SOCIETY   KENTUCKY DEPARTMENT OF HIGHWAYS   2231

In the summer of 1841 when Lincoln's on-again, off-again romance with Mary Todd dictated a change of scenery, Abe made an extended visit at the home of his friend, Joshua Speed. The Speed home, Farmington, on the outskirts of Louisville, looks today much as when Lincoln visited there.

both men. When the legislature convened in December, Lincoln would be in the state capital, Vandalia.

But other things were going on in the meantime. Seemingly every day, some judgment was lodged against the Lincoln/Berry store enterprise. Although Lincoln had two steady jobs and was paid for other assorted chores, such as election clerk, he simply could not cope with the debt. Accordingly, on November 19, 1834, his surveying equipment and horse were taken to be auctioned in settlement of a debt. New Salem resident and Lincoln's friend James Short won the bidding for Lincoln's equipment at $120 and promptly gave it back to Abe. Short reports that Lincoln repaid every cent.

On November 28, along with the three other district representatives, Abe Lincoln departed for Vandalia clothed in a brand new $60 custom-made suit. The seventy-five mile trip required a little over twenty-four hours as he arrived at 4 PM on the next day. A friend named Coleman Smoot had loaned Mr. Lincoln $200 to buy the suit, get his creditors off his back and pay his expenses at Vandalia until he was paid as a legislator, which would probably be around Christmas.

Abraham Lincoln was duly sworn in and took his seat as a legislator on December 1. In the housekeeping necessary to begin a session, he was appointed to the Committee on Public Accounts and Expenditures two days later, but his name appears so seldom in the reports that we can only conclude that he was content to watch, listen and learn. Among the men he met there was Stephen A. Douglas and many others who were to become prominent in state and national politics. In his autobiography, Lincoln states that at this juncture, his friend Stuart, who was a lawyer, encouraged him to study law and offered to lend his books.

As New Salem was an entirely different social world

from Gentryville, so Vandalia was another notch up the scale. One can only imagine the social whirls which enveloped the rookie representative in the parties, restaurants and boarding houses of the Illinois Capital. To help that imagination along, the old State Capitol is still there for us to see and tour, and many of the houses in town look much as they probably did when Mr. Lincoln was there.

The legislature worked through Christmas, holding sessions on the 24th and 26th and finally adjourned in February. A more confident Lincoln made his way back to New Salem, perhaps with some of Stuart's law books under his arm. This experience in the legislature had afforded Lincoln an opportunity to measure himself against the most knowledgeable and powerful men in the state. By his own admission, he found himself wanting in education, but, in reality, not wanting in intelligence, drive or ability.

There being no formal procedure for becoming a lawyer, the normal practice was for an aspirant was to make an arrangement to "read law" in an existing office. Many would-be attorneys had a family member already in the profession, and so had a built-in path. Abraham Lincoln had opportunity for neither of those options, so he read and studied by himself. So lank was he that no chair would comfortably accommodate his long legs, hence him lying on the ground with his back propped against a tree reading a book was a common sight. On several occasions, he walked the ten miles to Springfield to borrow another book. So we see that another of the Lincoln myths is true.

Surveying, serving as postmaster and studying law kept the young man busy between legislative sessions. As there were no lawyers any closer to New Salem than Springfield (10 miles), an aspiring lawyer had occasion to perform many of the more mundane legal duties – those chores we call "boilerplate" today – that would normally befall one reading law more formally. These chores included drawing up wills, land title work, leases, contracts, bills-of-sale and the like. Abe performed these duties and sometimes even argued cases before the local justice of the peace. As he was not licensed as an attorney, he was not allowed to charge anyone for such services, but it was valuable experience.

One experience stuck with Lincoln long after it was over, for he learned how the law could be tempered by common sense. He was arguing a case, Ferguson v. Kelso, contesting ownership of a hog before his friend, justice of the peace,

Bowling Green. Lincoln made a powerful argument – as he always did – and presented witnesses proving the hog belonged to his client, Ferguson. When the arguments were finished, Squire Green declared that the witnesses were "damned liars" and, as "the court being well acquainted with the shoat in question," from his own knowledge, he knew the hog belonged to Kelso and so ruled.

There were other distractions, as well. Sometime in 1833, a Kentucky belle named Mary Owens showed up in New Salem to visit her sister, Mrs. (Elizabeth) Bennett Able. As Lincoln was a friend of the family, he met Miss Owens there. She was from a rich family, was refined and cultured, in short, quite the opposite of the awkward, uneducated and poor Mr. Lincoln. Despite these differences, Lincoln seemed to be taken with her, but was romantically occupied with Ann Rutledge. A year or so after Ann's death, Elizabeth Able informed Lincoln that she was to make a visit to her relatives in Kentucky and that she would bring her sister back if Lincoln "would engage to become her brother-in-law with all convenient despatch (sic)." Lincoln evidently felt honor bound to accept that challenge, but confided to a friend that he "was most confoundedly well pleased with the project."

Sure enough, Mrs. Able returned to New Salem, twenty-eight year-old sister Mary in tow. Lincoln himself says he was appalled at the change in her appearance since he had last seen her. "When I beheld her, I could not for my life avoid thinking of my mother; and this, not from withered features – her skin was too full of fat to permit of its contracting into wrinkles – but from her want of teeth, weather-beaten appearance in general and a kind of notion that ran in my head that nothing could have commenced at the size of infancy and reached her present bulk in less than thirty-five or forty years." That's honest Abe talking!

Nonetheless, Lincoln felt honor bound to attempt to marry her. And so he did, struggling to find reasons to love her. He admits that he delayed his duty as long as possible, finally popping the question in the fall of 1837. Imagine, if you can, the tall, awkward Lincoln ratcheting up his courage, asking and then standing waiting, anxiously dreading her effusive acceptance. Then imagine his relief when she refused him!

Human nature being what it is, Lincoln then suffered from the rejection, concluding that in his efforts to find

something worthy of his love in her, he had managed to love her a little. "But," he concluded, "let it go."

Mary Owens eventually returned to Kentucky where she married a man named Vineyard in 1842. In her correspondence with Herndon following Lincoln's death, she described a particular incident in which Lincoln had displayed what she considered indifference toward her as an example of why she refused to marry him. She also initially denied that she told Lincoln he would not make a good husband but in a later letter said that, indeed, she did tell him so. She concluded to Herndon, "I thought Mr. Lincoln was deficient in those little links which make up the great chain of a woman's happiness, at least it was so in my case…." And she did say that she and Mr. Lincoln remained friends. In fact, her cousin related that she had two sons in the Confederate Army. Mary told him she would not have hesitated to appeal to the President had her sons needed Presidential help.

For his part, after some self-castigating for having made such a fool of himself, Mr. Lincoln wrapped up the affair this way: "…I have now come to the conclusion to never again to think of marrying, and for this reason – I can never be satisfied with anyone who would be blockhead enough to have me." That was 1838, a year or so before he met another Kentucky Belle, Miss Mary Todd.

Part IV

The year of 1836 brought great changes in Lincoln's life. In March, he announced his candidacy to return to the legislature. He ran on the Whig ticket as one of seventeen hopefuls (7 Whigs and 10 Democrats) including his future brother-in-law, Ninian Edwards. At the same time, friend and future law partner John Stuart announced his candidacy for the United States Congress.

Before any campaigning began, another milestone occurred when, on March 24, the name of Abraham Lincoln was entered on the books of the Sangamon Circuit Court certifying him as "a person of good moral character," the first step in becoming a licensed attorney. On the same date, he purchased two lots on the north side of Jefferson Street in Springfield.

As archaic as the informal process of becoming a lawyer seems in these days of LSAT's and bar exams, there is something to be said for the way it was done in Lincoln's day. At least one person – usually a judge – had to certify that the aspirant was "of good moral character." Given the general reputation of lawyers today, an argument could be made for reinstating that rule.

In the election campaign, the candidates traveled over the district – Sangamon County was as large as Rhode Island – to the various venues and usually all appeared together, speaking in turn until all had been heard. On one such occasion, July 30, in Springfield, one of the Democratic candidates made some charges that Ninian Edwards deemed untrue. Edwards jumped up on a table and, at the top of his voice, declared the charges false. Intense excitement ensued, and there was talk of a duel to settle the issue. Lincoln, next to speak on the program, took up the issue at hand, handling the dispute so adroitly that "everyone was astonished, and pleased. So, the difficulty ended then and there." In attendance that day was Joshua Speed, yet another Kentuckian living in Illinois, who was to become Lincoln's best and only true friend.

"Gentlemen and fellow citizens; I presume you all know who I am. I am humble Abraham Lincoln and I have been solicited by many friends to become a candidate for the legislature…
–Lincoln

His stance on the issues of the day was consistent, advocating "all sharing the privileges of the government, who assist in bearing its burdens," and "admitting all whites to the right of suffrage, who pay taxes and bear arms, by no means excluding females." He also always declared his loyalty to the Whig Party's commitment to internal improvements and ended, "If alive on the first Monday in November, I shall vote for Hugh L. White (the Whig candidate) for President."

On Monday August 1, the entire Whig ticket was elected – a remarkable result in a district which had previously been entirely Democratic – with Abraham Lincoln receiving the highest number of votes among the 17 candidates for representative. As it happened, each of the seven Whig representatives and two senators was over six feet tall, hence the group became known as "The Long Nine."

The Whigs did not fare so well in the November Presidential election. Although White carried the New Salem district and Sangamon County, the remainder of Illinois and the country disagreed, sending Democrat Martin Van Buren to the White House.

On September 9, 1836, two justices of the Illinois Supreme Court certified that Abraham Lincoln was licensed to practice law in all Illinois jurisdictions. Lincoln surely was duly proud; that certification was the culmination of much hard work and study. He was not long in beginning his actual law career; the Sangamon Circuit Court session began on October 3, Judge Stephen Logan (a future Lincoln law partner) presiding. Lincoln had his first case two days later. His appearance in court is apparently despite the fact that he had not yet satisfied all the requirements to practice law. After the "good moral character" and the Justice's recommendation for license, the statues specify that aspirants appear before the clerk of the Supreme Court for enrollment. Lincoln did not comply until March 1, 1837, so evidently the enrollment was a mere formality.

The Tenth Illinois General Assembly held in the winter of 1836-37 was one of the most important in the State's history. In his first legislative session, Lincoln had been content to listen and learn. Now, buoyed by that experience and the recent election triumph, he was ready to assume a leadership role. Under his leadership, "The Long Nine" guided the legislature, acting on the will of the people to implement the Whig principles, voting into place plans for railroads, widening of every important river and stream, and a plan to build a canal from the Illinois River to Lake Michigan. They then authorized the State to borrow $12,000,000 – a staggering sum – to fund these programs. Additionally, the issue of moving the state capitol having been under discussion, The Long Nine managed to have the seat of government moved to their district, specifying Springfield as the new Capital. Finally, they addressed both of the burning issues concerning slavery. The General Assembly passed a resolution stating that "we highly disapprove of the formation of Abolition societies and of the doctrines promulgated by them," and that "the right of property of slaves is sacred to the slaveholding

States by the Federal Constitution, and that they cannot be deprived of that right without their consent." Remember that many, if not most, of the residents of Illinois were born Southerners.

Just before the session ended, Lincoln, morally opposed to slavery, but aware of the political ramifications, wrote a protest to the above resolution, but could induce only one other member of The Long Nine to sign with him. In a carefully worded protest, Lincoln wrote into the Illinois House Journal:" …[We] believe that the institution of slavery is founded on both injustice and bad policy, but that the promulgation of abolition doctrines tends to increase rather than abate its evils," and " [We] believe that the Congress of the United States has no power under the Constitution to interfere with the institution of slavery in the different States." Years later, when Lincoln was running for President, those who called him an Abolitionist had evidently not read that protest when he wrote it nor heeded its repetition in his autobiography with the comment that his position on slavery "was then (in 1837) the same as it is now (1860.)"

As winter melted into spring, Lincoln found that he had outgrown New Salem. The little village had not lived up to the hope that it would become a booming river port and, indeed, would soon wither and blow away. Fortunately for us, much of it was rebuilt in the 1930's, so we can see how it looked in Lincoln's day.

While New Salem withered, Lincoln thrived. Uneducated as he was, he was the most knowledgeable person in the town, often called upon to arbitrate disputes with his knowledge, fairness and unstinting honesty. Those qualities were now known, not only locally, but throughout the State, and his statewide reputation also included recognition as a skillful politician.

New Salem had been as good for Lincoln as he had been for it. Nearly every resident was uneducated and had humble origin, so these were not handicaps. Equal opportunity was more of a fact at that time at that place than all the modern laws can make it now. Abraham Lincoln was a man who, having taken full advantage of those opportunities, found it was time to move on.

At left: Lincoln poses in the park across from the "old" State House in Vandalia, IL. He served only one term in this building, constructed in 1836.

SPRINGFIELD

1837 - 1860

Where it is: In Central Illinois between St. Louis and Chicago, about 100 miles northeast of St. Louis.

How Lincoln got there: Rode in from New Salem on a borrowed horse.

How you get there: Interstate Highway 72 or 55.

Part I

Having tried farm laborer, boat hand, boat owner, river pilot, store clerk, store owner, surveyor, postmaster and politician/legislator, by the spring of 1837, Abraham Lincoln had settled on the latter as his occupation. Although his education was self-inflicted and deficient and he had little practical experience, he knew that New Salem was no place for a lawyer. Always one to take advantage of an opportunity, and, as he had had a hand in moving the State Capitol to Springfield, what better place to hang out his shingle? Once the state offices came to that city, the state and federal courts would not be far behind, so a lawyer there would have occasion to practice at those levels as well as the circuit court and hence get to associate with the "shakers and movers" of the day.

Upon arrival in Springfield with all his clothes and a couple of law books packed in his saddle bags, Lincoln sought out Joshua Speed, the Louisville native he had met during the previous political campaign. At the time, Speed owned a store and assisted in editing a Springfield newspaper. Lincoln entered the store, saddlebags in hand, to inquire about lodgings. After some conversation, Speed informed Lincoln that he had a large room with a double bed, "which you are perfectly welcome to share with me if you choose."

Where is your room?" Lincoln asked.

"Upstairs," Speed answered, pointing to the stairwell. Speed reports that without a word, Lincoln took his saddle bags upstairs, tromped back down the steps and "with his face beaming with smiles, announced, 'Well, Speed, I'm moved.'"

On April 15, 1837, *The Sangamo Journal* announced: "J. T. Stuart and A. Lincoln, Attorneys and Counsellors (sic) at law, will practice conjointly in the courts of this Judicial Circuit." Law partnerships were much less formal in those days, forming and dissolving as the needs of the men involved changed. In this instance, Lincoln's Black Hawk War and legislative friend John Stuart had failed in his bid for the U.S. Congress the previous fall, but planned to try again, so he needed a junior partner to take care of the practice while he was away. Lincoln, with no experience and no clients, needed the established client base and advice that a senior partner would offer.

Almost immediately, Lincoln began appearing in court, mostly on behalf of clients Stuart had already scheduled. Most of the cases were routine, but one suspects that Lincoln began to discover how lacking his legal education actually was. Still, years later, he advised a young man, "If you are resolutely determined to make a lawyer of yourself, the thing is more than half done already. It is but a small matter whether you read with anybody or not....Get the books and read and study them until you understand them in their principle features....The books, and your

Lincoln and Billy Herndon occupied offices in this building on Springfield's public square opposite the 'new' state house.

capacity for understanding them, are just the same in all places," he showed that he did not consider the method of his education as faulty. When Lincoln's son Bob started to law school, the father commented, "You may get a better education that I did, but you won't have as much fun."

Stuart and Lincoln were fairly busy with routine lawyers chores for the next year or so. Divorce was fairly common in those days and accounted for a part of their cases, but creditors suing for default on credit notes was much more prevalent as were are boundary disputes. These disputes had Lincoln and Stuart in court nearly every day throughout 1837 and 1838.

Despite the hectic court schedule and political activities, Lincoln is lonely! It is difficult to imagine the gregarious story-teller feeling alone, but in a letter to Mary Owens, he wrote, "This thing of living in Springfield is rather a dull business; at least it is so to me. I am quite as lonesome here as I ever was anywhere in my life. I have been spoken to by but one woman since I have been here, and should not have

been by her if she could have avoided it. I've never been to church yet, and probably shall not be soon."

And there were other activities, too. If it's difficult to picture Abraham Lincoln in a lonely situation, try this one, reported by his friend and room-mate Joshua Speed. Among Billy Herndon's papers at the Library of Congress is this, one of several stories he collected but did not find fit to print, clearly to protect his lamented partner's legacy. In an 1889 interview Speed told Herndon that during the period he and Lincoln roomed together, he (Speed) "was keeping a pretty woman" in Springfield. "Lincoln, desiring to have a little said to Speed, 'Speed, do you know where I can get some?' In reply, Speed said, 'Yes, I do and if you will wait a moment or so, I'll send you to the place with a note. You can't get it without a note or by my appearance." According to Speed, Lincoln took the note and went to see the lady in question.

"Things went right on," continues Speed, "Lincoln and the girl stript (sic) off and went to bed." Before things went

Lincoln and Herndon had this view of the State House from their office.

further, Lincoln asked the lady how much she charged. At her reply of $5, Lincoln informed her that he only had $3. After she offered to trust him for the balance, Lincoln said, "No, I do not wish to go on credit." As Lincoln got out of bed and was getting dressed, the lady said, "Mr. Lincoln, you are the most conscientious man I ever saw." When Lincoln returned to his room, Speed says that they had no conversation about the matter. Years later, Speed told Herndon that he learned the details a few days later when he had occasion to visit the lady and she told him all that was said and done. On his notes concerning this incident, Herndon added, "I have no doubt of its truthfulness."

Lincoln's living with Speed has caused much speculation that he may have been homosexual. This incident certainly damages that speculation. That same summer the previous legislative session's authorization of state debt began to rear an ugly head. The situation became so dire that the governor called a special session of the legislature to convene July 10. Just before he left, Lincoln attended an Independence Day celebration which included laying the cornerstone for the new Springfield State House.

Although it was totally unknown to Lincoln, Mary Todd of Lexington made her first visit to Springfield that summer of 1837. Her sister, Elizabeth Edwards, the wife of Ninian Edwards, another one of the Long Nine, had invited her for the summer. Miss Todd heard, of course, of the tall ungainly partner of her cousin, John Stuart This man Lincoln, she was told, was an effective stump speaker, could put up forceful logical argument in court, was fond of the company of women but shy around them and unwaveringly honest. Despite those connections and however her curiosity may have been piqued, her time was consumed by relatives and friends, dances and receptions. Likewise, Mr. Lincoln was surely aware of the vivacious,

witty, politically astute, attractive "Kentucky belle" in Springfield's society. Nonetheless, Mary Todd and her future husband passed the summer without meeting; in the fall, she went home to Kentucky and he went to Vandalia.

When the General Assembly convened, the Whigs put Lincoln up for Speaker of the House, but, being in the minority party, he did not win, although the losing margin was but one vote. Governor Duncan's purpose in calling the session was to ask the legislature to help quell the pending financial panic by repealing the internal improvements acts passed the previous fall. Not surprisingly, the lawmakers refused to amend their own work. They were to pay for that obstinacy at the next election.

Lincoln was undeterred, however, by these developments. On February 24, 1838 he announced his candidacy for the general assembly once again. For the same election, Lincoln's partner, Stuart, was a candidate for the United States Congress, his opponent being Stephen A. Douglas. The campaign between those two began amicably enough in April, but soon turned violent, resulting in a physical fight a few days before the August election. On August 6, Lincoln was once again returned to the General Assembly with the highest vote among the 17 candidates, and Stuart beat Douglas by 36 votes from the 36,495 votes cast – a margin of less than 1 percent.

Early in December, Lincoln took a break from his almost daily court appearances to return to Vandalia for the General Assembly session. Once again, he was nominated for Speaker of the House and once again, a Democrat – the majority candidate – was elected. Perhaps as a boon to the harried legislators, an eight mile section of track was completed on the Northern Cross Railroad and the first locomotive west of the Alleghenies and north of the Ohio River made a trial trip amid great ceremony – a small return for the vast expenditures they had allocated.

Illinois was growing in population and, so were the legal problems. As more people poured into the frontier state, new counties were carved from the existing ones creating new courts and new circuits. When Lincoln and Stuart first became partners, Sangamon county was in the First Judicial District, one of the five existent at the time. Therefore, there was not a lot of need for the circuit riding that would later become such a big part of Lincoln's law practice.

At this point in Abraham Lincoln's life, he probably thought he was pretty well settled. He was, indeed, well established in his law practice, recognized state-wide as an able politician, respected and admired as an honest, clear-thinking, affable citizen and a pillar of the Springfield community. At thirty years of age, he had parted ways with his father, buried a sister and a brother and his mother and endured two ill-fated romantic affairs. Surely, a full life up to this point, but the next few years had plenty of changes in store for Mr. Lincoln. Some of these changes were foreseeable; Stuart would be going to Washington, the State Capitol was coming to Springfield, and he would take undisputed leadership of the General Assembly. But, Dame Fortune had a few unpredictable tricks up her sleeve, too.

Part II

Sometime in October 1839, Miss Mary Todd returned to Springfield, this time to live permanently with her sister. Born in Lexington, Kentucky on December 13, 1818, she was the daughter of Robert S. Todd, one of the leading citizens and politicians in Kentucky. All the leading lights of the day – Henry Clay, John C. Breckenridge, Charles Morehead and Simon Buckner as well as generals, cabinet members, jurists, governors and presidential candidates were regular visitors to the Todd home on Main Street. Mary not only knew them all, but listened to the talk and heard, from "the horses' mouth" their political philosophies and gained a political education the like of which could not be had elsewhere. As a matter of fact, Mary Todd said that she was a Whig from age fourteen when her friend, Henry Clay ran against Andrew Jackson for President. She was educated in more traditional ways as well. She had attended schools in Lexington where she learned to speak French and English with equal fluency, the gentle ways of an elegant lady and to float as lightly as a butterfly across a dance floor. Not particularly beautiful, but attractive and charming enough, she was an immediate factor in Springfield society, just as she had been on her visit two years previously. After her mother died, Robert Todd had remarried. Most historians agree that "Molly" had come to a parting of the ways with her step-mother, and wanted to get out of her father's house. In her biography of Mary Lincoln, Emilie Todd Helm's daughter, Katherine, who got

all her information from her mother, vows that is not so. Apparently the second Mrs. Todd made a great distinction between her step-children (including Mary) and her natural children (including Emilie), so it is not surprising that Mary and Emilie had different views of the second Mrs. Todd. At any rate, another Todd sister, Frances, who was living with the Edwardses married Springfield physician William Wallace. This development "created a vacancy in the family," so Mary had come to seek her future in her sister's home.

The fact was that Mary Todd did not like Billy Herndon, considered him an alcoholic, rude and uncouth and suspected his motives as concerned her husband's future. After her marriage, she refused to invite him to her home. This was not lost on Mr. Herndon. As history unfolds, Billy, as Lincoln's biographer, got the final word and he has been accused of putting it to good use, paying Mrs. Lincoln back in spades for her dislike of him. Herndon said that the future Mrs. Lincoln "was a very shrewd observer, and discretely and without apparent effort kept back all the unattractive elements in her unfortunate organization." Many of Springfield's residents would not have disagreed with that assessment. To be fair, Herndon did give her what was due as a caring compassionate wife and mother. Mary's sister, Elizabeth, had a kinder view: "Mary was quick, gay, and in the social world somewhat brilliant. She loved show and power and was the most ambitious woman I ever knew. She used to contend, when a girl, to her friends in Kentucky that she was destined to marry a President. I have heard her say that myself, and after mingling in society in Springfield, she repeated the seemingly absurd and idle boast." Mrs. Edwards added that her sister made that remark "in all seriousness."

Lincoln knew the Edwardses, of course. Mary's brother-in-law, Ninian, was a member of Lincoln's Long Nine, and Lincoln was a frequent visitor in the Edwards' home. Lincoln's friend Joshua Speed was also intimate with the Edwardses, so Abe and Mary were bound to meet. It happened at one of the many social functions in Springfield that winter of '39, and they were attracted to each other right away. It is easy to see why he was taken with her wit, knowledge of politics, conversational ability and charm. In fact, Elizabeth Edwards reports that Lincoln was "charmed by her wit and fascinated by her quick sagacity."

The other side of the equation is not so clear. Perhaps she saw Presidential timber in the ungainly Lincoln, perhaps his attentiveness was the major factor, but she did seem equally taken with the aspiring politician.

There is a story that the evening they met, Lincoln approached Miss Todd and informed her that he "would like to dance with her in the worst way." Later, she told her sister, "And he did, too." Maybe so, but that does not ring true as Lincoln was well aware of his physical awkwardness and at White House functions assigned someone to dance with his wife.

What Mary saw in Lincoln was certainly lost on her sister. "He was a good, honest and sincere young man whose rugged, manly qualities I admired," says Mrs. Edwards, "but to me he seemed somehow ill-constituted by nature and education to please such a woman as my sister." She did not hesitate to tell Mary that Lincoln, in her opinion, was not brother-in-law material. Lincoln, of course, was aware of Elizabeth's opinion of him.

At the same time, Miss Todd was seen walking the board sidewalks of Springfield arm in arm with Lincoln's political – and now apparently romantic – rival, Stephen Douglas. Perhaps she saw more apt Presidential timber in Douglas, or maybe she was attempting to create some fervor in the undemonstrative Abe, but if it was a ploy, it did not work. None took such a romantic link-up seriously – Miss Todd and Mr. Douglas – an ardent Democrat – were too different politically to ever agree on much.

Nonetheless, the courtship continued and soon reached the engagement stage. Some time in 1840, Lincoln gathered the Kentucky belle in arms and asked her to marry him. She agreed and the family started making plans. How either of the couple actually felt was known only to themselves. But, In December, Mary Todd wrote a friend telling of another lady who "appears to be enjoying all the sweets of married life," and yet another friend who was on the verge of "perpetrating the crime of matrimony."

Lincoln, the circuit-riding lawyer, was at work, riding through the rain, sleet and snow, eating poorly cooked meals at irregular intervals and sleeping in drafty, noisy boarding houses. Speed reports that by the time Lincoln returned to Springfield, his nerves were shot. One evening, Lincoln approached his friend Speed, a letter addressed to Mary Todd in his hand. Handing it over, he asked Speed

to read it. Speed said that in that letter, Lincoln made a plain statement of his feelings and, having spent great deliberation of the matter, admitted that he "did not love her sufficiently to warrant her in marrying him." Lincoln asked Speed to deliver the missive to Miss Todd. Speed refused and threw letter in the fire, telling Lincoln that he had better be man enough to go tell her to her face that he did not want to marry her.

Promising to do as instructed, Lincoln left on his unhappy errand. Speed waited downstairs more than an hour until his friend finally returned. One can imagine the forlorn look on Lincoln's face and Speed's anxiety as he pressed for the details of the meeting. "Well, old fellow," said Speed, "did you do as you promised?"

"I did," Lincoln replied, no doubt with a sigh. "She burst into tears and nearly sprang from her chair crying something about the deceiver being deceived." He paused.

"Well?"

"To tell you the truth, Speed, it was too much for me." Lincoln then related how, with tears streaming down his own cheeks, he took her in his arms, kissed her and renewed his pledge to marry.

Here, the reports diverge. Some say that the above conversation took place on January 1, 1841 while other reports indicate whenever the conversation occurred, what Lincoln was to call "the fatal January 1" was the date fixed for the wedding. The January 1 reconciliation version relates that – however reluctantly – the Edwardses began to redecorate the house, invite guests, plan the meal and arrange the furniture. Then, when the appointed time arrived, while Mary waited in the bedroom, the bridegroom failed to appear. The other story is that long before the wedding day, Mary saw how miserable Lincoln was and subsequently released him from his promise. Mary's sister, Elizabeth, told Herndon that "everything was ready and prepared for the wedding," but Mr. Lincoln "failed to meet his engagement." Before Herndon's papers became publically available, some historians (and, most notably, Mary Todd's family) accused him of inventing that story, but it is what Mrs. Edwards told him. Given what we know of Mr. Lincoln's character, it is difficult to see him agreeing to the wedding and then just not showing up. Elizabeth Todd Edwards, whatever her motivation, created the controversy when she told Herndon a different story than she told the family. In her biography of her aunt, Mary's niece, Katherine Helm, says that her mother (Emilie Todd Helm) "declares Herndon's story to be absolutely false and a cruel reflection on the character of a noble man...."

At any rate, the engagement was definitely off and Mary did write Lincoln a letter so stating and releasing him from his pledge.

There's an additional twist on this romantic scene. Cyrus Edwards of Alton came to Springfield in November 1840 for the legislative session. With him came his daughter Matilda. As cousin of Ninian Edwards, Matilda moved into his home where Mary Todd was already living. Here, Matilda and Lincoln met and the Edwardses told Herndon that Lincoln's love for her was the cause of the Lincoln-Todd break-up. Perhaps he did love her, but if so he never mentioned it to her. All accounts agree, however, that Mr. Lincoln told Mary Todd that he loved Matilda. The Edwards' credit that remark to his "insanity" while Speed and Springfield friend James Matheny insist that he meant it.

Rumors flew through the Springfield social circles: one camp said that Mary Todd had jilted Lincoln; another that after all her flirting with Stephen Douglas, Lincoln had decided that their marriage was not good for either, while yet another rumor had her now engaged to Stephen Douglas. Neither party bothered to verify or deny any of the rumors, evidently content to allow the townsfolk to think whatever they liked. Apparently, however, Lincoln was devastated. A couple of weeks later, he came down with a malady which he termed "hypochondriasis" that confined him to his bed for a week during which only Joshua Speed and his doctor, Anson G. Henry, saw him. When finally he did emerge from his room, he was not the same man, appearing "reduced and emaciated" and so weakened as to "scarcely to possess strength enough to speak above a whisper." The Edwardses and many other locals were convinced that Lincoln had lost his mind.

To be sure, the care-free, merry story-teller was gone. Lincoln's friends hid razors and all sharp objects for fear he'd harm himself. As so he himself indicated in a letter to Stuart on January 23, 1841, that indeed he might: "I am now the most miserable man living. If what I feel were equally distributed to the whole human family, there would

not be one cheerful face on the earth. Whether I shall ever be better, I cannot tell; I am awfully forbode I shall not. To remain as I am is impossible; I must die or be better, it appears to me."

Mary Todd was apparently on the other end of the scale. From all appearances, which she ensured Lincoln saw, she was on a merry whirl of feminine activity. "She (Mary) accompanied a large party on the railroad cars to Jacksonville last Monday," Lincoln wrote Speed, "and on her return spoke, so that I heard of it, of having enjoyed the trip exceedingly. God be praised for that!" Another Springfield resident made an observation of the show: "Miss Todd and her cousin (Mrs. Edwards) seem to form the grand center of attention."

While all the romantic activity was going on, life continued in other aspects. Lincoln had court cases and legislative sessions to attend, although his name is often missing from the House Journal indicating that he was absent and that he said and did little when he was present. In November of 1839, his law partner, John Stuart had gone to Congress leaving his junior partner to handle the business. Lincoln noted the event by heading a new page in his office journal, "Commencement of Lincoln's Administration." Perhaps he had gained enough experience under Stuart's guidance to handle the legal work, but he did miss his partner's knowledge of the accounts. Soon after Stuart's departure, Lincoln wrote him "about some little matters of business. You recollect how you told me that you had drawn the Chicago Musick money & sent it to the claimants? A damned hawk-billed Yankee is here, besetting me at every turn I take, saying that Robert Kinzie never received the $80 to which he was entitled. Can you tell me anything about the matter?" That letter shows some of Lincoln's exasperation and indicates that he did not consider himself a "Yankee" perhaps revealing something of his Kentucky heritage as well.

Also, the population of Illinois had exploded to the point that the five existing Judicial Circuits were not sufficient to meet the legal needs of the citizens. Accordingly, four additional circuits were created, and Springfield was placed in the newly created Eighth Judicial Circuit. At the time,

"I have never seen the prospects of our party so bright ..."
—Lincoln

the Eighth covered a huge area, eventually encompassing seventeen counties – about one-eighth of Illinois. Traveling from one venue to another was a problem, not only from lack of roads, but also due to vast unpopulated areas which offered a circuit rider no food or shelter. Nevertheless, there were those attorneys who enjoyed the circuit riding. Abraham Lincoln was one of them.

For one thing, court day in every county was a combination festival and circus. Everybody who could flocked to town whether he or she had court business or not. Knife swapping, horse trading and social gatherings were all a part of the action. As other forms of diversions were scarce, the actual courtroom action also served as entertainment. So, the lawyers and judges were the "rock stars" of the era, and it may be that Lincoln enjoyed that status as well. Another attraction, for Lincoln anyway, was the companionship and camaraderie. The attorneys, judges and sometimes litigants were usually acquainted. When the day's business was finished, the whole crowd would adjourn to the nearest tavern where the drinking and story-telling would begin. Lincoln didn't – not ever – drink alcoholic beverages, but he could, and did, imbibe on the yarn-swapping with the best of them. Having the other attorneys and judges for "drinking buddies" did no harm to his political career, either.

One of the other lawyers gives us a glimpse of life on the circuit. "The way we traveled was thus: Lincoln, Swett, O.L. Davis, Lamon, Drake, myself (lawyers) and Davis (David, Eighth District Judge) would ride from Urbana to Danville in livery rigs – take a day – 36 miles; sing & tell stories all the way; stop at a farm house & wait for them to kill and cook chickens for our dinner; get to Danville at dark. Lamon would have whiskey in his office for the drinking ones; those who indulged in petty gambling would get by themselves & play until late in the night. Lincoln & Davis & a few local wits would spend the evening in Davis' room talking politics, wisdom and fun." Another attorney reports that after inquiring into Lincoln's whereabouts one evening, he was informed that the gentleman could be found in Judge Davis' room. Approaching the door with the gravity and decorum due a judge, he rapped lightly. "In response to my timid knock, two voices responded almost simultaneously, 'Come in.' Imagine my surprise when the door opened to find two

men undressed, or rather dressed for bed, engaged in a lively battle with pillows, tossing them at each other's heads." While such entertainment was certainly not to be had at home, there's certainly no mention – not even a hint – of escaping from wives in those scenes.

He was not always absent from Springfield during these years. As expected, the Federal and Illinois State courts moved to the new capital city. Lincoln is admitted to practice in the United States Court on December 3 (1839) and argued his first federal case a few days later. Illinois' General Assembly held its first Springfield meeting December 9 at the Second Presbyterian Church, the new State House not yet being ready.

As if Mary Todd, court cases and circuit riding and the General Assembly weren't enough to keep Mr. Lincoln busy, the Whigs kicked off their 1840 Presidential election campaign nearly a year in advance of the election, bypassing Henry Clay as their candidate for once and announcing a ticket of William Henry Harrison and John Tyler. "Tippecanoe and Tyler too" were opposed by the Democrat, Martin Van Buren. The Whigs had no platform other than being opposed to all things Democratic, but a newspaper soon gave then a battle cry when it noted that Harrison "would be content if somebody would give him enough money to live on and a log cabin with plenty of hard cider." So, despite the fact that Harrison was comfortably wealthy and well educated, the national campaign became "the log cabin and hard cider" candidate versus Van Buren "an aristocrat who eats his meals from gold plates and drinks his champagne from crystal goblets." So ridiculous did the canvass become that a Springfield Democratic editor noted that he was "surrounded by log cabins on wheels, hard cider barrels …" so that " if a sober Turk were to drop among us, he would be induced to believe we were a community of lunatics…." Lincoln, nonetheless, campaigned for Harrison and Tyler, making stump speeches with his usual logic and skill and worked tirelessly behind the scenes for his party, organizing the state into districts and checking on the local chieftains. His speeches were usually answered by Stephen Douglas; sometimes the two traveling together to a speaking venue. Additionally, he kept his absent partner advised, telling Stuart, "I have never seen the prospects of our party so bright …" although he thought his own chances of reelection were "not flattering" as he "may not be permitted to be a candidate."

Lincoln did not seem too disappointed by the prospect that he might not be reelected. When the session adjourned in February, he wrote Stuart that the assembly "had accomplished nothing of importance." Perhaps the affairs of the heart were distracting his attention, but he seems to have lost his enthusiasm for law-making.

When election day arrived in the fall of 1840, Illinois remained solidly in the Democratic column while the nation went for the Whig ticket of Harrison and Tyler in a big way. Despite Lincoln's trepidation in the matter of his own legislative future, he was resoundingly reelected to the House.

In June of 1841, Mary Todd indicated to a friend that she was not quite as carefree as she seemed and did not consider that all relations between her and Lincoln were over. "The last months have been of interminable length," she lamented. Then, referring to Lincoln, added, "…The prairie land looks as beautiful as it did in olden time, when we strolled together and derived so much happiness from each other's society."

In Lincoln's "miserable" letter to Stuart, (January 23, 1841) he had implied that a change in their partnership arrangement might be in order and indicated that Doctor Henry had advised a change of scenery. Lincoln declared that he would go to South America if Stuart could secure a consular post for him. When newly inaugurated Whig President William H. Harrison died in office, all chance of Stuart's procuring the appointment was lost, so some other change would have to be instituted. Whether or not Stuart's failure to help was a factor in the break-up of the partnership is problematical, but when Stuart returned to Springfield in April, Lincoln turned over the money owed from the firm's earnings and the partnership was dissolved. Soon, a new partnership between Lincoln and former Judge Stephen T. Logan was announced.

The solution to the "change of scenery" was provided by Joshua Speed who, following his father's death, had sold his store and moved back to Kentucky sometime early in 1841. In August, Lincoln went to visit the Speed mansion, Farmington, near Louisville. While there, Lincoln hung around the Jefferson County Courthouse and Joshua Speed's brother, James' law office. In December 1864,

President Lincoln would appoint James Speed as U.S. Attorney General.

If Lincoln came to Kentucky for diversion, he found it. Not only did he read James' law books and talk politics – they were all solid Whigs – but had some other adventures as well. As Lincoln returned to Farmington one evening, probably from James' office, three muggers descended upon him, a long silver knife blade gleaming in the moonlight dangerously near Lincoln's throat. "Could you loan a man $5 on that?" demanded one of the men. Although Lincoln was physically strong, he was wise too and thought discretion the better part in this instance. Pulling the only bill he had with him from his pocket, he said, "Here's $10 neighbor. Put away your scythe."

At the time, Joshua Speed was courting a lovely dark-haired, dark-eyed young lady named Fanny Henning. Speed would make any excuse to see his girl, including taking Lincoln on a trip to Lexington, simply so they could stop in to see her on the way home. Usually, much to the young lovers' chagrin, they could never escape the company of her uncle, John Williamson, with whom she lived. "Uncle John" was an ardent Whig who always wanted to talk politics with Speed, never leaving the couple any time alone. As "Uncle John" and Lincoln had never met, when Lincoln accompanied his friend to the Williamson home, he pretended to be a Democrat. "Uncle John" got so involved in argument with his "Democratic" guest that he forgot about his niece for a while, allowing the couple an uninterrupted evening. Speed and Fanny were soon engaged and he credited Lincoln's dramatics as being a key factor. No record is left of what Lincoln and "Uncle John" talked about, but it would surely have been interesting to hear Abe's "Democratic" arguments.

One other incident occurred while Lincoln was visiting, and the memory of it stayed with him. One morning when no one else was around, Speed's mother, Lucy, observing the crestfallen and miserable disposition of her lanky Illinois visitor, presented Mr. Lincoln with a Bible. Perhaps also knowing that to this point in his life, Lincoln had exhibited no interest in religion, she advised him to read it and that by obeying its precepts, he would "obtain a release from his trouble which no other agency could bring him." We do not know if he took the lady's advice, but on October 3, 1861, President Lincoln did send her an autographed picture of himself inscribed, "For Mrs. Lucy G. Speed from whose pious hands I accepted the present of an Oxford Bible twenty years ago." In 1866, Speed told Herndon that his mother, then eighty years old, valued that picture "above all price."

Most who knew Abraham Lincoln, in his later years at least, say that he never confided in anyone and that he never asked anyone's advice. Anyone who said that clearly was not aware of the relationship which developed between Lincoln and Joshua Speed from their meeting in 1836, their rooming together until Speed left Illinois and through the summer and fall of 1841 in Louisville. The surviving letters between the two men reveal a deep friendship and abiding trust in each other's judgment.

As Lincoln's spirits lifted, Speed came down with the same indecisiveness that had plagued Lincoln. While the Speeds never saw Lincoln as "insane" as had been suggested, the two friends now swapped roles as it was Speed who began to have misgiving about his proposed marriage. The two traveled to Springfield together, leaving on September 7, 1841. "Nothing of interest happened on the passage," wrote Lincoln, but he did remember seeing a dozen slaves "chained together like so many fish on a trot-line." Perhaps his views on slavery were crystallizing, as a full decade later, he remembered the incident, writing Speed that, "the sight was a continual torment to me and I see something like it every time I touch the Ohio." The two men arrived in Springfield a week later, just in time for the opening of circuit court.

As Lincoln dove back into his law practice, Speed hung around for a while, leaving on or about January 1, 1842. Lincoln sent him away with a letter to be read on the journey. In it, Lincoln, in his new role as counselor of affairs of the heart, told Speed that he understood why Speed was indecisive, "… it is an apprehension that you do not love her as you should. What nonsense!" Pressing the point and telling Speed (and us) of his own malady, he noted, "You know the hell I have suffered on that point…."

Upon arrival back in Louisville, Speed found that his intended, Fanny, was ill and that fact evidently helped crystallize his feelings, as marriage plans were finalized straight away. On the eve of Speed's wedding, Lincoln wrote, speaking of the end of Speed's need for his advice on the matter, and assured his friend, "… in two or three

months, to say the most, (you) will be the happiest of men."

In mid-February, Joshua Speed and Fanny Henning were married and Lincoln sent his congratulations and revealed his true feelings on the friendship: "I shall be very lonesome without you … if we have no friend, we have no pleasure…." Evidently he meant what he said; in another letter the same day, he expressed envy and perhaps revealed some of his hope for reconciliation with Mary Todd. "…it is the particular misfortune of both you and me to dream dreams of Elysium far exceeding all that anything earthly can realize." A month later, Mary Todd was very much on his mind when he told Speed that his (Speed's) last letter, "gave me more pleasure than I have enjoyed since that fatal first of January 1841. Since then, it seems to me that I should have been entirely happy but for the never absent idea that there is one still unhappy whom I have contributed to make so. That kills my soul…."

The idea that bitterness existed between Mr. Lincoln and Miss Todd is evident in Lincoln's correspondence with Speed through the summer and early fall of 1841. In June, Speed advised Lincoln that he should either marry the lady or get her out of his mind. The next month, Lincoln responded that "I must regain confidence in my own ability to keep my resolves when they are made." One wonders if he meant that he wished he had married her at the first opportunity, or wished he had the determination to stay away from her.

Sometime in late August or September, Mrs. Simeon Francis, wife of the *Sangamo Journal's* editor, and Lincoln's doctor, A. G. Henry, conspired to invite Abe and Mary to a social function. Mrs. Francis subsequently told Herndon that "a marriage between a man as promising in the political world as Lincoln and a woman as accomplished and brilliant in the social world as Mary Todd would certainly add to the attractions of Springfield…. "Each showed up, unaware that the other would be there and evidently they took the advice to heart when Mrs. Francis encouraged them to "be friends again." The couple then began meeting – in great secrecy – at the Francis' home. Even Mary's sister, Elizabeth Edwards, was initially unaware of the reconciliation, probably because Mary was fed up with hearing her sister's opinion of the marriage.

In September, Mary Todd and her friend Julia Jayne published a series of letters in the *Sangamo Journal* lampooning the Democratic State Auditor, James Shields. Shields fancied himself quite the ladies man and had apparently somehow managed to incur the wrath of Miss Todd. Abe Lincoln had a hand in the poem, perhaps in composing it and almost certainly in assuring its publication. The letters smacked of the biting wit of Miss Todd, but as Lincoln and the *Journal's* editor, Simeon Francis were staunch political allies, Lincoln had virtual free reign of the pages of the newspaper. Purporting to be written by a widow who called herself "Aunt Becca of Lost Townships," she poured bitter satire on Shields in one letter, then changed her tune in the next. She described herself as "not over sixty, just four-feet-three in my bare feet and not much more around the girth" and ended with a proposal to marry Shields. Incensed, Shields demanded the name of the author

"I shall be very lonesome without you …if we have no friend, we have no pleasure…."
–Lincoln

from the paper's editor. He may have suspected Lincoln was involved anyway, but when Lincoln instructed Francis to give Shields his name with no mention of the women, Shields challenged Lincoln to a duel. In his answer to Shield's initial communication, Lincoln demonstrated his logic and command of the English language. "…without stopping to inquire whether I really am the author, or to point out what is offensive in them, you demand an unqualified retraction of all that is offensive and then proceed to hint at consequences….the consequences to which you allude would be a matter of great regret to me as it possibly could be to you." Lincoln told a friend that he did not desire to kill Shield, but nonetheless accepted the challenge as a mater of honor. As he had the choice of weapons, Lincoln, perhaps tongue in cheek, selected "cavalry broadswords of the largest size available." When they arrived at the designated spot across the Mississippi from Alton, Shields' friends, considering the height and wingspan of the lanky adversary, evidently had second thoughts and the matter was bloodlessly resolved "with honor to all concerned." As far as Abraham and Mary were concerned, the whole "Lost Townships" affair was evidently an adventure and drew them closer.

That something was going on is evident in Lincoln's

October 5 letter to Speed: "I want to ask you a close question. Are you now in *feeling*, as well as *judgment*, glad you are married as you are? From anybody but me, this would be an impudent question, not to be tolerated; but I know you will pardon it in me." Then with a note of urgency, Lincoln closed, "Please answer quickly as I am impatient to know."

Evidently, Speed assured his friend that marriage was wonderful. Speed later told Herndon that he was sure that "if I had not been married and happy – far more happy than I expected to be, Lincoln would not have married."

Mr. Lincoln and Miss Todd had planned to be wed in the minister, Dr. Dresser's home. On an early November morning, Lincoln met Ninian Edwards on the street and advised him of the plan. Edwards insisted that the wedding take place at his home. On Friday morning, November 4, 1842, Lincoln showed up at the room of his friend, James H. Matheny, who was still in bed. Informing his sleepy friend that he was to be married that evening, Lincoln requested that Matheny be his best man. About the same time, Miss Todd was making a similar request of her "Aunt Becca" collaborator, Julia Jayne. That evening in the Edwards' home, Abraham Lincoln, "as pale and trembling as if being driven to slaughter," and Mary Todd were united in holy matrimony.

Such arrangements as could be made on the short notice included the invitation of only a few friends, one of whom was elderly Supreme Court Judge Thomas C. Brown. When Lincoln repeated, amid a perfect hush, the vow "with this ring I thee endow with all my goods and chattels, lands and tenements," the Judge, evidently unaccustomed to such formality, remarked in a voice loud enough for all to hear, "Lord Jesus Christ, Lincoln, the statute fixes all that!" On the ring that he slipped on her finger, he had inscribed, "Love is Eternal." A report exists that Mary removed the ring a few days before she died. When her sister Elizabeth found it, she said it had "AL to Mary Nov. 4, 1841 Love is Eternal" inside. Elizabeth put the ring back on her sister's finger so that Mary was buried wearing her wedding ring.

Why the haste to "tie the knot" leaves some vexing questions. In his entire lifetime, Lincoln had only one true friend, Joshua Speed. Speed was in Louisville, but why was there was not time to summons him to Springfield to act

as best man? Was Lincoln afraid she'd back out? Elizabeth Edwards, who seems to be the villain, noted that "even a serving girl would have given the family enough notice to bake a cake." Given the social standing of the Todd girls, one would think that they would have scheduled weeks of gatherings honoring the bride and groom. But, no. Was she afraid he'd change his mind again? The reason for the the rush is another of those things we'll never know, but we can be sure that Elizabeth Todd Edwards was a factor.

Speed assured Herndon that Lincoln married Mary Todd strictly from a sense of honor, an assessment with which Herndon personally agreed, readily accepted and heartily endorsed. Hence, in his Lincoln biography, Herndon pulled no punches on the matter: "…at last he stood face to face with the great conflict between honor and domestic peace. He chose the former, and with it years of self-torture, sacrificial pangs, and the loss forever of a happy home." It must be remembered that Herndon had no social intercourse with Mrs. Lincoln and Mr. Lincoln discussed his affairs with no one. Hence it follows that all Herndon knew of Lincoln's home life was mere gossip. But, even if Herndon was correct, it still does not explain the urgency. Much has been written concerning Abraham Lincoln's martial happiness, but a glimpse into that and perhaps the emergency of the nuptials is provided by the lady who would know, Mary Lincoln: "Mr. Lincoln's maxim and philosophy was, 'What is to be will be and no cares of ours can arrest that decree.'"

Part III

After the Friday evening wedding, on Saturday, the newlyweds moved into the Globe Tavern where $4 per week bought room and board. If there was a honeymoon, it took place on Sunday as Lincoln was in court representing the firm of Logan and Lincoln on Monday, November 6. These arrangements were probably a financial necessity as Lincoln was still paying off his "national debt" of New Salem days.

Although busy with the firm's law cases, his political ambition did not wane, despite the fact that he had grown weary of the Illinois General Assembly. Still a die-hard Whig, he spoke in public at every opportunity and

supported every party candidate. By the spring of 1843, Abraham Lincoln had his sights on the United States Congress. This was not to be for a while yet, as evidently the local Whigs had set up a rotation system under which the four men considered qualified would wait their turn. The 1842 nomination went to John Hardin. In 1844, despite Lincoln's efforts to gain it, the nomination went to Lincoln's friend Edward D. Baker (after whom the Lincolns were to name their second son) who was elected in August. Finally, in 1846. Lincoln's turn came. This "rotation" arrangement, Lincoln later explained, was to "keep peace among our friends and to keep the district from going to the enemy." So, for the next few years, Abraham Lincoln could concentrate on his marriage and his law practice.

One could not say that he did so patiently. Abe Lincoln was not one who let anger show through very often, but he was not happy when the party locals refused him the nomination for Congress in '44 and then appointed him as delegate to the nominating convention, expecting him to support the Whig candidate. Lincoln's chagrin was evident

when he wrote Speed that he felt "a good deal like a fellow who is made a groomsman to a man that has cut him out and is marrying his own dear gal."

The Lincoln's first son, Robert Todd (Bob) was born in the Globe Tavern in August 1843. In the fall, needing more room, the Lincolns moved to a small house at 214 South Fourth, but stayed only a short time. By January 1844, attorney Lincoln was earning a good income. His debt was under control and the family was growing, so they needed more space. They purchased a small story-and-a-half house at the corner of Eighth and Jackson Streets paying the Rev. Charles Dresser, the man who performed their marriage ceremony, $1500. After son Eddie was born in 1846, a downstairs bedroom was added. Abraham and Mary Lincoln lived in this house, adding more space as necessary, until they went to the White House in 1861.

Much speculation has been written indicating that Lincoln's wife pushed him into political office as he personally had no political ambition. Anyone, then and now, who believes that is unaware that the man himself

Lincoln's home on the corner of Eighth and Jackson Streets. The National Park Service says that the "Quaker Brown" is the original color, but Mary Lincoln's "Little Sister," Emilie Todd, says the house was white with green shutters when she was there in 1854.

The Lincolns would probably feel right at home in their bedroom as restored by the NPS.

wrote a friend, "Now if you should hear anyone say that Lincoln don't want to go to Congress, I wish you, as a personal friend of mine, would tell him that you have reason to believe that he is mistaken." Mrs. Lincoln, being an intelligent woman and having grown up in a highly charged political household no doubt had her own opinions and no doubt shared them with her husband. Therefore, it is not much of a stretch to credit her with having helped shape some of his policies, but, by his own admission, he wanted the offices for which he ran.

In another letter, Lincoln detailed some of the campaign tactics which cost him the 1844 nomination. One of these was that he was labeled as the "candidate of pride, wealth and aristocratic family distinction," evidently referring to his wife's family. Lincoln said that those who knew him as a "friendless, uneducated, penniless boy" would be "astonished if not amused" by that classification. Another of the attacks on him was that "no Christian ought to go for" Lincoln because he belonged to no church. These tactics make it difficult to understand why Lincoln should name his second son after the man who leveled those charges, even if the latter charge was certainly true.

While Lincoln and partner Logan complemented each other in many ways. Logan was everything Lincoln was not: orderly, studious and thrifty and knew the technical aspects of law. The partnership was good for both men at the time it was formed in 1843. Two years later though, Lincoln thought he had learned all he could from Judge Logan. When the two became rivals for the same political post, it was time for the partnership to end.

When Lincoln first came to Springfield, a young man named William – "Billy" to all who knew him – Herndon was a clerk in Joshua Speed's store where Lincoln lived until his marriage. Hence, Lincoln and Herndon were well acquainted and somewhere along the line Billy began a formal study of law. Although there is no evidence that Lincoln assisted him, evidently they liked each other, so he probably lent Billy a hand here and there. In the court records for November 27, 1844, in Lincoln's handwriting, over the Circuit Judge's signature is the certification that William H. Herndon is "a person of good moral character," the first step, as we have seen, to becoming a lawyer. Herndon satisfied the remainder of the requirements

and was admitted to the bar on December 9. By that time, Lincoln had remedied some of the deficiencies he identified in his education and was ready to become the senior partner in a law firm. Accordingly, before the end of the year, the firm of Logan and Lincoln was dissolved and Lincoln and Herndon became an entity that was to last until the end of the senior partner's life.

With his political career on hold and Billy Herndon to do the "boilerplate" work of the law office, Lincoln had time to tend to his family – son Robert Todd was born in 1843 and son Edward Baker in 1846 – and his law education. He studied the law books to fill in the gaps in his knowledge. Still a ravenous reader, he also found time to study Euclid's Geometry, Shakespeare and some poetry, too. He also studied all the humor and joke books he could lay hands on. Anyone who was ever around Abe Lincoln spoke of his ability to come up with a humorous parallel to almost any situation, He did not possess that ability innately, but rather worked at committing any amusing story he read to his marvelous memory against the time he could use it appropriately.

The 1844 Presidential election saw Whig Henry Clay run against Democrat James K. Polk. The major campaign issue was the annexation of Texas (which had been an independent entity since 1836 when the Texans defeated Santa Anna's army), Polk in favor and Clay opposed. Needless to say, Lincoln stood with Clay on the issue and tirelessly stumped all of Illinois and some of Indiana on Clay's behalf. While in the Hoosier State, he had the opportunity to visit some old friends from his Gentryville days, but that's about all he accomplished. Both states fell into Polk's column. Election returns, amid accusations of slander and vote fraud, showed Polk with 170 electoral votes to Clay's 105, despite a very small popular majority. Subsequently, Polk took office and Texas was indeed annexed by the United States in 1845.

When 1846 rolled around, Lincoln still wanted to go to Congress, and it was his turn for the Whig nomination. His Democratic opponent was a well-known circuit riding Methodist minister, Peter Cartwright. As Cartwright lived near New Salem, he and Lincoln were old adversaries. The minister made not even the least effort at separating church and state. He had preached and campaigned in nearly every Methodist church in the district and used

his extensive family connections as well. Intelligent and quick-witted, Cartwright won most arguments and surely expected to win the election.

Cartwright's supporters pointed to Lincoln's lack of church participation and accused him of "the grave offense of infidelity," a charge that Lincoln was hard-pressed to deny in any truthful manner. Billy Herndon says that Lincoln abandoned the law practice entirely, leaving his partner to carry on while he actively campaigned across the district.

One evening during the campaign, Cartwright was preaching in a town where Lincoln had made a political speech in the afternoon. Perhaps thinking his opponent might allude to the canvass under way, Lincoln slipped into a back pew and listened quietly to the minister's denunciation of slavery, whiskey, Whiggery and the devil, not necessarily in that sequence. In conclusion, Cartwright leaned forward and asked all who expected to go to heaven to stand. Everyone rose except Abe Lincoln. Somewhat taken aback, the preacher then asked everyone who expected to go to hell to rise. Lincoln kept his seat. Infuriated, Cartwright pounded the pulpit and fired point blank, "May I ask, then, where Mr. Lincoln expects to go?"

Slightly embarrassed, Lincoln slowly rose to his feet. By the time he reached his full height, he was ready to answer. With just a hint of a smile, he drawled, "Why, Preacher, I expect to go to Congress."

Campaigning was a bit cheaper in those days than now. The local party contributed $200 in expense money early in the canvass. After the election, Honest Abe gave back $199.25, explaining that at one rally a group of farmers had insisted that he buy them a seventy-five cent barrel of cider.

On election day, August 3, 1846, the voters of the Springfield district made it clear that, however popular Cartwright might be personally, they believed in separation of church and state and hence did not want a preacher in Congress. Although Lincoln voted for Cartwright, Mr. Lincoln was elected, receiving the highest Whig vote ever recorded in the district. Other than Lincoln's election, the Whig ticket had little to celebrate either nationally or locally; Lincoln was the sole Whig elected in Illinois. Lincoln himself evidently found the result somewhat disappointing as he told Speed that, "being elected to Congress ... has not pleased me as much as I expected."

The Congressional session was more than a year away, leaving plenty of time for gathering his constituents' views and preparing to go to Washington. A major issue was presented when the Mexican War began in April before Lincoln's election. As Congressman-elect, he had to declare his position and did so in a Springfield speech on May 29, 1847. Historically, during a war the opposition party has always had difficulty finding ways to attack the administration in power while still displaying patriotism, but Congressman Lincoln had no such problem. He stated that he stood with his party in opposition to President Polk's war of aggression. Now that the United States was in a war, however wrong the motivation might be, patriotic loyalty demanded that he declare his support for the troops. If that sounds familiar, it is just one more pointer to the fact that things don't change much in the world of politics.

Before the Lincolns left for Washington, they decided to pay a visit to the Todds in Kentucky. The *Illinois Journal* (formerly the *Sangamo Journal*) announced the departure with the opinion that "He will find a good many men in Congress who possess twice the good looks and not half the good sense." The three weeks spent in Lexington would be the first vacation of Lincoln's life. Abe and Mary, with Bob, age 4 and Eddie at 18 months in tow, left Springfield on October 25, 1847 and met Joshua Speed in St. Louis on the 27th. Evidently, there was time for a visit with his old friend as the Lincolns arrived at Mary's father's home on November 2. As they traveled by boat via the Ohio, Mr. Lincoln no doubt relived many of his boyhood adventures as they steamed along with the Indiana bank on one side and Kentucky on the other. Reaching the mouth of the Kentucky River, they turned, heading to Frankfort and then rode by rail to Lexington.

This would be Mary Lincoln's first homecoming since she went to Springfield eight years previously. While her father had visited in Illinois during that period, her step-mother and three step-siblings had never set eyes on Mary's gangly husband. Likewise, the Lincolns did not know Mrs. Todd's nephew, Joseph Humphreys, who was on

"Why, Preacher, I expect to go to Congress."

—Lincoln

the train from Frankfort with the Illinois visitors. As the Todds' coachman picked up the Lincolns' luggage, young Humphreys walked to the Todds' Main Street home. Bounding up the steps, he addressed Mrs. Todd, "Aunt Betsy, I was never so glad to get off a train in my life! There were two lively youngsters on board who kept the whole train in a turmoil and their long-legged father, instead of spanking the brats, looked pleased as Punch and sided with and abetted the older one in mischief."

Just at that moment, the Todd's carriage pulled up in front of the house. Looking out the window, young Humphreys cried, "There they are now!" The nephew, who was just the first of many to complain of Abraham Lincoln's tolerance of his boys' behavior, fled the room and was seen no more in the Todd home while the visitors were in town.

Mary Lincoln's little half-sister, ten-year old Emilie, thought the tall stranger was the giant from Jack and the Beanstalk. She later wrote that as he stooped to pick her up, she "expected to hear 'fe, fi, fo, fum'" but instead he lifted her saying, "So this is Little Sister." "Little Sister," she was thereafter, even when she came to the White House in 1864 after the death of her Confederate General husband.

During the visit, Lincoln hung around the Fayette County Court House. No doubt, he noticed the slave auction blocks in the yard, perused Robert Todd's extensive library, talked with some of the old folks about his forbearers who had lived in the vicinity, made friends with Mary's brother, Levi and observed domestic slavery at close range in the Todd household. As Ashland, home of Lincoln's political idol, Henry Clay, was just out the other end of Main Street, the Lincolns probably paid the "Great Compromiser" a visit.

Lincoln probably also noted that in Lexington, just as at home in Springfield, many of the leading citizens were missing – with the Army in Mexico. Henry Clay, who had recently lost a son in the Mexican War, was to speak out against "Mr. Polk's War" on November 13. Putting his personal grief and whatever bitterness was left over from the previous Presidential campaign aside, Clay delivered a masterful argument against the war, and surely found a receptive audience in the Whig Congressman from Illinois.

Just before their departure for Washington, Abe and Mary attended the Presbyterian Church where they heard the great minister and slavery opponent, Robert J. Breckenridge, speak. Lincoln left no record of any impression the Reverend Breckenridge made on him, but he surely did not realize how important the minister would be when President Lincoln was struggling to keep Kentucky in the Union.

Washington DC

Lincoln, with his wife and children, departed Lexington on November 25, 1847. They probably took a stage coach to Winchester, Virginia where they could make a railroad connection to Harper's Ferry from where the Baltimore and Ohio had a branch line to Washington. There is no record of any disturbance that the boys made anywhere on this journey, and they arrived and checked into Brown's Hotel late in the evening of December 2.

Lincoln did not record his impressions of "Washington City," but he was probably surprised to find the nation's Capital nearly as primitive as Springfield. Only a few streets were paved in 1847; sidewalks were mostly ashes and the few street lights shed their smoky light only when Congress was in session. The White House looked much as it does today, but the Capitol still had its old, wooden dome. Some 37 churches probably were losing the battle against the many saloons, gambling houses and bordellos which lined the streets.

Four days after arrival, Abraham Lincoln was sworn in as a Member of Congress and took his seat as the Gentleman from Illinois. Busy before Christmas, he wrote Herndon to say that "as you are so anxious for me to distinguish myself, I have concluded to do so before long." There was routine business to attend to first: he was appointed to two standing committees and moved the family to Mrs. Sprigg's boarding house in Carroll Row on Capitol Hill where the Library of Congress is today.

Despite the fact that all major battles of the Mexican War were over before Congress convened, the war's causes and effects were still the hot topics in the Thirtieth Congress. The Whigs maintained that President Polk had started the war "unnecessarily and unconstitutionally" despite Polk's message to Congress contending that Mexico had struck

Washington's Pennsylvania Avenue as it looked in Lincoln's day. Library of Congress

the first blow. Back in Illinois, Mr. Lincoln had been able to declare Party loyalty and still remain relatively quiet on the issue, but now, he had to choose a side. When another of the Illinois members (obviously a Democrat as Lincoln was the "Lone Whig") introduced a resolution declaring the war to be "just and necessary," Lincoln, along with the rest of the Whigs, voted "no."

On Wednesday, December 22, the "Gentleman from Illinois" rose to "distinguish" himself as he had promised Herndon he would. He proposed a series of resolutions, the first of which demanded that the President name the spot where the Mexicans spilled the first blood of the war. Other resolutions in the series asked the President if that spot was in territory taken from Mexico by Texas and so on. Not surprisingly, Lincoln's proposals became known as "The Spot Resolutions." Also not surprisingly, President Polk used the power of his office to ignore the questions.

So serious was the Whigs' objection to the War that

when Congress voted a resolution of the nation's thanks to hero Zachary Taylor, they added the phrase "In a war unconstitutionally and unnecessarily begun by the President" to the verbiage.

For once, the politically astute Lincoln had misjudged his ground. The Whigs in Congress might have been opposed to the War, but the folks back in Sangamon County certainly were not! At first, the newspapers chided Lincoln for not honoring the heroes who had fought and died south of the border, but the criticism soon turned more harsh, accusing him of "having placed a stain on the patriotism and glory" of Illinois. Herndon wrote regularly to inform his partner of attitudes at home and early on hinted that re-nomination might be in the offing, but that hope soon wilted under the disparagement. So seriously did the criticism impact Lincoln that as late as his 1860 campaign autobiography, he was still defending his stance on the Mexican War.

Hon. Abraham Lincoln. Library of Congress

At the end of the first session, in the spring of 1848, Mary Lincoln and the boys left smelly, smoky Washington for the fresh air at her parents' home in Kentucky. Some of the letters exchanged between Abe and Mary have been preserved, giving us some insight into their relationship. Had Billy Herndon had access to those missives, he might have revised his estimate of his partner's marriage. His first letter to her begins: "In this troublesome world, we are never quite satisfied. When you were here, I thought you hindered me some in attending to business but now, having nothing but business – no vanity – it has grown exceedingly tasteless to me." After some chatty news, he teased her a little, "I am afraid you will get so well and fat and young as to be wanting to marry again…." and signed off, "Most affectionately, A. Lincoln." That does not sound like a man who is relieved to be rid of his wife.

Robert Todd owned a summer house he called "Buena Vista" on the Frankfort Pike outside Lexington. The site, in Franklin County, is now on a golf course. From that venue Mary wrote a long personal and social update, and lamented, "How much I wish, instead of writing, we were together this evening, I feel very sad away from you." She signed her letter, "My love to all, truly yours M.L." In the same light, that does not sound like a woman who is happy to be back in her hometown.

Much has been written indicating that Mary Lincoln was embarrassed by her husband and hence was always trying to correct him in some way. His request, "Suppose you do not prefix the 'Hon.' to the address on your letters to me any more. I like the letters very much, but I would rather they should not have that upon them" indicates not only his humility, but that she was proud of his status.

Besides the war, the other burning issue in the late 40's politics was slavery. Mr. Lincoln had already made his views clear on the topic, and his record in Congress did not change his thinking. Personally opposed to slavery, he contended that the nation should not allow the "peculiar institution" to spread to new territories. At the same time, he was politically astute enough to let slavery be in the places where it already existed. The nation was so split on the issue that the question of whether slavery be allowed to spread even crossed party boundaries; each side found allies in both parties, the division being more geographical than political.

By the time the second session of Congress began in December 1848, that issue was about to come to a boil, settling down only when the Compromise of 1850 allayed it. Congress did consider, and Lincoln did vote for, a law appropriating money from the sale of public lands to compensate all slave owners who would free their slaves. Obviously, Congress did not approve the measure.

Lincoln and Congress were disinclined to interfere with slavery in states where it already existed. The District of Columbia, however, was a bird of a different feather. The 40,000 residents (of which 10,000 were slaves and free blacks) had no vote, so the political dangers of addressing state's rights were nonexistent in the nation's Capital. Lincoln voted against

Mary Todd Lincoln. Library of Congress

two proposals concerning the DC slaves, probably because he had a plan of his own in the works. On January 10, 1849. Congressman Lincoln announced his plan to introduce a bill which would confine slavery in the District to those who were already there. Also, under his plan, children born of slaves in the District after January 1850 would be free. Any District slave owner who desired to free his chattel would be paid a fair market value by the Untied States Government. Finally, and most controversially, the plan also provided for the apprehension and return of fugitive slaves entering the District. Lincoln said that his plan was subject to approval by a vote of the residents of the District. Should the residents vote in his plan, it would be immediately effective. On January 13, he declared his intention to put his proposal in the form of a bill, but for reasons known but to himself, he did not do so.

In the spring of '48, when we all know where all young men's fancy went, all Congressmen's thoughts turned to the upcoming Presidential election. Internally, the Whigs loved their chief, Henry Clay, but as he had already failed to be elected four times and the only time a Whig had been elected was 1840 when Clay was passed over for the nomination, the party leaders cast about for another candidate. As has happened several times before and since, a military hero emerged as a likely vote-getter. General Zachary Taylor had earned his reputation in what the Whigs called "an unconstitutional and unnecessary and damnable war," was a slave owner, favored the annexation of Texas– all opposite Whig principles. Additionally, he had shown no previous interest in politics, but appeared electable. So, on the qualification of being popular, he was duly nominated by the Whig party. Faithful to his Party, as always, Lincoln worked hard to nominate and then elect Taylor, "not because I think he will make a better President than Clay, but because I think he would make a better one than Polk, Cass or Buchanan."

In a letter to Billy Herndon, he urged his partner to organize the local voters for Taylor. Billy was a little discouraged, however, partly because of local attitudes on Lincoln's opposition to the war and the fact that the young Whigs were upset "at the stubbornness and bad judgment of the old fossils in the party." In passing, history again demands the mention that General Taylor was future Confederate President Jefferson Davis' father-in-law.

The outlook for the Whigs dimmed some in August. Due to the rotation arrangement (if not disappointment in his performance) Lincoln was not re-nominated, the honor going instead to former partner, Stephen Logan who was subsequently soundly defeated in his bid for Congress. It would appear, then, that Logan, not Lincoln, paid the price for Lincoln's unpopular Congressional performance.

As summer turned to fall, Lincoln soldiered on for the Party. Instead of joining his wife and sons in Kentucky as planned, he began a speaking tour of New England. That he was an accomplished speaker by this time was reported by the *Boston Advertiser* following his speech at Worcester, "He spoke in a clear and cool, and very eloquent manner, for an hour and a half, carrying the audience with him in his able arguments and brilliant illustrations." Perhaps the most significant aspect of the campaign for Lincoln personally was the opportunity to hear William Seward when the two spoke from the same platform in Boston. Seward, currently a New York Senator and former Governor, was just beginning to emerge as the leader of the anti-slavery wing of the Whig Party.

"In this troublesome world, we are never quite satisfied. When you were here, I thought you hindered me some in attending to business but now, having nothing but business — no vanity — it has grown exceedingly tasteless to me."
–Lincoln

When the tour ended, Lincoln began a winding journey home to Springfield via Albany, Buffalo and Niagara Falls. Back home, he tried to drum up support for Taylor in Illinois. Still, his record on the war haunted him. A Northern Illinois newspaper reported, "Lincoln has made nothing by coming to this part of the country …. He had better have stayed away." Small wonder he was still defending his stance on the Mexican War when he ran for President twelve years later. Despite his efforts, Illinois again went into the Democratic column, but Abe Lincoln was delighted when Zachary Taylor was elected President of the United States on November 7, 1848, carrying the Springfield district by 1500 votes.

Returning to Washington for the second session of Congress in December, Lincoln found little to excite

his interest and, in the spring, his career as a Member of Congress ended in a whimper. Evidently, though, the Illinois Whigs felt that he was due some reward for his services and also that the office of Commissioner of the Land Office should go to a resident of their State. Accordingly, Lincoln was asked to apply to President Taylor for the post. In typical self-depreciating fashion, Lincoln declared that there were others better qualified, but that he would accept the position, "if it becomes clearly impossible for any of the others to get it." In the end, that appointment went to an Illinois resident who was not mentioned as one of Lincoln's "better qualified." That development was perhaps fortunate for Lincoln: four years at a desk in Washington would have not only put him out of touch with the voters, far out of his natural element interacting with "just plain folks."

Then, perhaps because Lincoln's name was already on his mind, President Taylor offered Abraham Lincoln the post as Governor of the Oregon Territory. Many Whigs, including Lincoln's former partner and friend John Stuart, encouraged him to take that position, assuring that Oregon would soon be a state and that Lincoln would then be its first Governor or perhaps Senator. He seriously considered the offer, thinking that he had already committed political suicide, but his wife put her foot down – they were definitely not going to Oregon. So, Mr. Lincoln quietly went back

Seeking refuge from political applicants, President-elect Lincoln retreated to a room above his law offices where he wrote his inaugural address on this actual desk.

to Springfield, where his friends and family were, and dove into the practice of his profession.

Springfield
Part IV

In an age when many of us think that "honest lawyer" is an oxymoron, we could use a few more like Abraham Lincoln. In some notes he prepared for a lecture on the law – but evidently never delivered – he advised that, "if you cannot be an honest lawyer, then you ought to be an honest something else." And he practiced what he preached, too. History leaves us a couple of examples.

Henry Shaw, a Beardstown lawyer relates that Lincoln came to his office one day to question him about a suit Shaw had filed against one of Lincoln's clients to enforce the performance of a contract. Shaw explained his position and showed Lincoln his proof. Lincoln expressed surprise that Shaw should be so frank, but stated he would do the same. He proceeded to agree that Shaw was in the right and that he (Lincoln) would so represent to the court when the case was called. When he did so, a deed for the land in question was awarded to Shaw's client without, as Shaw put it, "the value of the property being consumed in litigation."

Lincoln's habit of carrying his papers in his hat sometimes caused him to be unable to produce them at the right time. Rather than make an excuse for not promptly answering another lawyer's query, Lincoln straightforwardly explained, "First, I have been very busy in the United States Court; second, when I received your letter, I put it in my old hat and buying a new one the next day, the old one was set aside, and so the letter was lost sight of for a time." The nickname of "Honest Abe" is one that Mr. Lincoln earned every day of his life.

As Lincoln re-entered his law practice, he told Herndon that he had no right to share in the money Billy had earned while he was in Congress. Herndon replied that as Lincoln had taken him in when he was unknown and unlearned, he was more than willing to divide equally. So, the partnership resumed as if Lincoln had never been away. Although little political activity went on in Abe Lincoln's life for the next few years, his legal work – circuit riding and all – continued unabated. At a time when the fee structure

dictated that income depend on volume, specialties of law were unknown. Lincoln and Herndon handled appeals, foreclosures, trespass, will probates, personal injury, the occasional break in tedium provided by divorce and slander and some criminal actions.

A young man who was studying law in the offices of Lincoln and Herndon left us a graphic description of the place: "The office was on the second floor of a brick building on the public square, opposite the court house.... There was one long table in the center of the room and a shorter one running in the opposite direction, forming a T, and both were covered with green baize....In one corner was an old-fashioned secretary with pigeon-holes and a drawer, and here Mr. Lincoln and his partner kept their law papers."

In the summer of 1849, an outbreak of cholera struck Central Kentucky. Although Robert Todd had taken his family to the summer home, Buena Vista, he had business which required his presence in town every day. Early in July, he contacted the dreaded disease and died on the 16th. Mr. Todd had just written a will leaving the bulk of his estate to his wife and the remainder to his children, "to be divided equally in just proportions" between those from his first and second marriages. Mary Lincoln's youngest brother, George, appeared at probate, objecting to the will as it had only one witness instead of the two the law required. As the will was then invalidated, the court ruled that the entire estate be divided equally among all the heirs! This ruling meant that the Widow Todd would have to sell all her husband's assets – including his interest in the firm of Oldham, Hemmingway and Todd – and divide the proceeds with her husband's fourteen children.

There is no indication that any of the four of Robert Todd's children who lived in Springfield took any part in invalidating the will, but as they were in the thick of it now, and as Abraham Lincoln was an able lawyer, they seem to have appointed him to look after their interests.

For reasons other than the will problems, the Todd estate needed a lawyer. So, in mid-October, the Lincolns again traveled to Lexington. En route, on the 26th their boat became involved in a race up the Ohio with another boat. As the Lincolns' vessel was low on fuel, it pulled alongside a wood barge. Abe Lincoln shouted, "Come on, boys," jumped onto the barge and threw wood up like a deck hand

The reflection in a window adjacent to the Lincoln-Herndon office building shows the proximity of the State House.

until the steamer was refueled. Hopefully, he enjoyed that diversion, as there was no fun to be had in Lexington.

A year or so before he died, Robert Todd had filed a law suit against an old personal and political rival, Robert Wickliffe. The legal action was the result of a sordid and twisted tale too involved to record all the details here. Briefly, one of Todd's ancestors had fathered a child by an octoroon (one-eighth black) slave girl about 1816. Ten years later, the slave girl and her son were the property of the child's grandmother, who was a Todd relative, when she married Robert Wickliffe. Unknown to her, Kentucky law specified that the slave pair then became Wickliffe's property. Thus did Mary Lincoln discover that she had a kinsman "with the taint of Negro blood beneath a Caucasian skin."

Mary's brother, Levi, was living in the old Todd

Lexington residence which was on Short Street behind the courthouse. From there, Abe and Mary no doubt had an excellent view of the slave auctions as well as the slave pens where the merchandise was held for sale. This would have been an different view from the mildest form of slavery he had seen previously in the Todd home, and Kentucky was very much in turmoil over slavery at the time. It is more than probable that Abe Lincoln left Kentucky with slavery on his mind.

Early in November, the Lincolns left for home, arriving in Springfield on the 15th. Not long afterwards, Eddie, just short of his fourth birthday, fell ill with pulmonary tuberculosis. Despite the doctors' efforts to save him, the lad died on February 1, 1850. A week or so later, a poem, written by either Abe or Mary appeared in the newspaper. It begins:

Those midnight stars are sadly dimmed,
That late so brilliantly shone,
And the crimson tinge from cheek and lip,
With the heart's warm life has flown -
The Angel of Death was hovering nigh,
And the lovely boy was called to die.

Many historians credit Eddie's death as the beginning of the instability that would eventually lead to Mary Todd Lincoln's being declared insane. Certain it is that the death of the child plunged both mother and father into deep depression. This is one of the several factors Herndon evidently overlooked in his explanation of the causes of Lincoln's depression.

In the spring, perhaps thinking that a change of scenery would improve their mood, and with Mary's father's estate still pending, the Lincolns traveled back to Kentucky. In Robert Todd's library, Abe stumbled across a book, *"The Christian's Defense,"* which caught his attention because the author was former a Kentuckian, Dr. James Smith. After the book's publication, Dr. Smith had moved to Springfield, IL where he was now the pastor of the First Presbyterian Church and the very man who had so recently conducted little Eddie Lincoln's funeral service.

Before leaving Kentucky, Lincoln filed a suit on behalf of himself and brother-in-law Ninian Edwards in conjunction with the Robert Todd estate. The suit alleged that Mary and Elizabeth's brother, Levi Todd,

had undervalued some of Robert Todd's property, all of which, as might be imagined, was much in dispute. This act would soon bring Levi's wrath down on the two Springfield men.

When the Todd estate business was wrapped up, Lincoln left his wife and son and returned to Springfield where he promptly looked up Dr. Smith. The preacher lent Lincoln his personal copy of his book, which Lincoln had not been able to finish in Kentucky. Dr. Smith later commented that he found Lincoln "much depressed and downcast at the death of his son and without the consolation of the Gospel." In those days, one paid a "pew fee" rather than drop money in the collection plate, so from then until he went to the White House, Abe paid an annual pew fee in Dr. Smith's church. From this time, evidence of a religious faith became more prevalent in his writings, although he never joined his wife in becoming a member of the Church. Worth noting is the fact that Lincoln was in Lexington about the time that Henry Clay was lured out of retirement to travel to Washington, DC to quell the turmoil erupting over slavery. The result was Clay's finest moment, The Compromise of 1850 which supposedly settled sectional disputes over the spread of slavery. That five-pronged legislation admitted California to the Union as a free state (thereby disrupting the balance of free vs. slave states in Congress), redrew the boundaries of Texas, established Utah and New Mexico as territories, abolished slave trade (but not slavery) in the District of Columbia, and implemented a stronger fugitive slave law. With that, Abe Lincoln lost what little interest in politics he had left.

Evidence of Lincoln's depression and disillusionment is offered by the fact that on June 5, 1850, a newspaper put forth Abraham Lincoln's name as one who should be nominated for the upcoming term of Congress. In a published response, Lincoln said that he was flattered by the attention, but made it clear that he had no interest in the nomination.

President Taylor unexpectedly died in office on July 9. On July 25, at four o'clock at Springfield's city hall Lincoln delivered Taylor's eulogy. Perhaps with slavery still on his mind, he said "I fear the one great question of the day, is not now so likely to be partially acquiesced in by the different sections of the Union, as it would have been, could

General Taylor have been spared to us. Yet, … trusting to our Maker, and … to the great body of our people, we will not despair, nor despond." President Taylor was replaced in the White House by Millard Fillmore. When the 1852 election rolled around, the Whigs by-passed Fillmore in favor of the other Mexican War hero, Winfield Scott. Scott carried only Massachusetts, Vermont, Kentucky and Tennessee, so Democrat Franklin Pierce was elected.

While Lincoln did the bulk of the circuit work – he enjoyed and reveled in it – for Lincoln and Herndon, there were plenty of cases for both partners right across the street in Springfield. So, Abe was home much of the time and evidently he and Mary decided to expand the family after Eddie's death; William Wallace (Willie) Lincoln was born in the house on Eighth Street four days after Christmas, December 29, 1850.

The cycle of life affords birth and death. Early in January, Lincoln received a letter from Dennis Hanks' daughter, Harriett, (of whom we shall hear more) informing him that his father was very ill, that he was not expected to recover, and if Abe wanted to see his father he had better make the eighty-mile journey to Coles County. Abe replied via his step-brother John Johnson that he had not answered the letters because "it appeared to me that I could write nothing which would do any good," that his "business is such that I could hardly leave home now." He concluded, "I sincerely hope Father may yet recover his health; but at all events tell him to remember to call upon, and confide in, our great, and good, and merciful Maker; who will not turn away from him in any extremity." Thomas Lincoln died on January 17, 1851, at age 73, without seeing his son. Clearly Abraham Lincoln harbored no fondness for the treatment he had received at his father's hands. The man who had shown little religious conviction thus far evidently had decided to put some faith in "our good and merciful Maker." There we have some evidence of how Lincoln's attitude had changed since his talk with Dr. Smith.

On June 29, 1852, Lincoln's political idol, Henry Clay died. When Lincoln delivered the Springfield eulogy on July 6, he knew that the Whigs had been in difficulty since Clay engineered the Compromise of 1850 over the protests of the northern branch of the party. When Lincoln said that Clay's "primary and all consuming passion was … a

Lincoln's political idol Henry Clay stands in Statuary Hall in the United States Capitol.

deep devotion to the cause of human liberty," he may very well have realized that the death knell was also sounding for the Whig Party. Soon after Clay's death, many Whigs would temporarily become "Know Nothings," but the seeds that would soon sprout the Republican Party were landing on fertile soil.

When Mary returned to Springfield, life settled down inside the Lincoln house on Eighth Street. Much has been written about the relationship between Abe and Mary Lincoln and many tend to accept Herndon's assessment that Abraham was miserable. Of the fact that Mary had a volatile temper, there is no doubt, as many of the residents of Springfield, particularly tradesmen and house maids, have testified. That the couple sometimes quarreled is a given – most couples do. They also apparently disagreed on child management, Abe being very permissive – and sometimes encouraging – with his boys' rowdy behavior. On that score, Billy Herndon said "…but out of respect for Lincoln … I shut my mouth, bit my lip and left for parts unknown."

Sometimes, Abe did the same. When Mary was on a rampage, he would snatch up whatever of the boys happened to be handy and go for a long walk in hopes she would have cooled by the time they returned.

The aforementioned Harriett Hanks came to live with the Lincolns in her youth. Following Lincoln's death, she told Herndon some about her years in the Lincoln household, praising Mr. Lincoln as being "all that a husband, father and neighbor should be." As for Mrs. Lincoln, she simply said, "I would rather omit further mention … as I could say but little in her favor."

There are various stories, told by neighbors, of which only one person claimed to have witnessed, so who knows the truth? One person alleges that he saw Mr. Lincoln come home late one evening to find the door barred against him. In response to his knocking, Mrs. Lincoln, from an upstairs window, dumped a pot of water on him. Another maintains to have seen Abe shove his wife out the door shouting, "Get out, damn you, you make the house miserable."

On the other hand, there is plenty of evidence, some of which we saw in the 1848 letters, of an abiding fondness between husband and wife. Even her harshest critics – Herndon included – admitted that Mary Lincoln

was an excellent wife, mother and teacher – she "home schooled" her boys and mothered her husband as much as her sons. In fact, Abe, who had called her "Molly" (as she was known in her family) early in the relationship, called her "Mother" after the children were born. She occasionally called him "Father, "but more usually referred to him as "Mr. Lincoln." The isolated instances of marital disagreement, even if they are true, allow us to infer that the majority of the time passed between them peacefully enough. One Springfield resident, William Barton, often spoke of "large and pleasant evenings" at the Lincoln home where the couple did their share of entertaining in Springfield society.

Katherine Helm says that her Aunt Mary would watch for her husband and "when it grew time for him to come home, she would meet him at the gate and they would walk to the front door swinging hands and joking like two children."

No one knows the reason, but there is no photograph of the Lincolns' as a family in existence. There are plenty of photographs of Abe, quite a few of Mary, the famous one of Abe, wearing glasses, and Tad, some of Mary and the boys, but none of Mr. and Mrs. Lincoln together.

Ah, but what about the well-documented instances of her erratic behavior and insane jealousy when she was the nation's First Lady? Those surely happened, but it must be remembered that she had lost two sons, was assailed by Northerners as a "rebel spy" and by Southerners as a "traitor," and was probably well on the way to her equally well-documented mental instability.

Beyond doubt, Mr. Lincoln was not as polished in social graces as was his wife – she, after all, had the benefit of being raised in luxury in one of Kentucky's wealthiest and most prominent families with the advantage of education in the genteel arts. We may be pretty sure that Abe Lincoln was not taught to use a butter knife or a salad fork in Thomas Lincoln's "half faced" camp. Those who knew him – his wife included – said that whatever he lacked in social grace was made up for by his kindness of heart. In fact, one day shortly after the birth of the Lincoln's fourth son, Thomas, (who was born April 4, 1853) Mary Lincoln remarked to Billy Herndon that "people do not realize that the kindness in Mr. Lincoln's heart is as great as his arms are long."

The last Lincoln son, named Thomas for his grandfather and, perhaps Abe's long-dead sibling, had a large head and as he wiggled, he reminded his father of a tadpole. Hence, he became "Tad" for all his life. Tad was a delightful child; the fact that a deformed palate caused him to speak with a lisp only endeared him more to his parents.

In the spring of 1853, an event occurred which shook Lincoln from his toes to the top of his stove-pipe hat. Evidently while in Kentucky dealing with the Todd estate problems, Mr. Lincoln made some arrangement with prominent Lexington lawyer George B. Kinkead to look after his interests. On May 26, out on the circuit at Danville, Abe received a letter from Kinkead, forwarded from Springfield, informing him that Robert Todd's surviving business partners, Oldham and Hemmingway, had filed a suit against Abraham and Mary Lincoln and his bother-in-law and sister-in-law, Ninian and Elizabeth Edwards, alleging that they had collected $472.54 on behalf of the firm of Oldham, Hemmingway and Todd and simply kept the money!

Abraham Lincoln was a man who held his temper quite well and was hardly ever known to even raise his voice regardless of provocation. In this instance, for the first and only time in his life, his integrity and honesty were being questioned, and his fury is evident both in his answer to the suit and the letter accompanying it. Although he had until the August term of the Fayette County (Kentucky) court to answer, he sat down at once, wrote his answer and had it certified by the clerk of the Vermilion County (Illinois) court the next day. In his notarized answer he denied having collected any money on behalf of his father-in-law except that when Robert Todd visited Springfield in the autumn of 1843 "when and where respondent for the first time in his life, met him," Todd had told Lincoln that he (Todd) was owed $50 in charge of a Beardstown attorney and that if Lincoln cared to collect it, "he (Todd) desired respondent to take it and retain it as his own." Warming to the challenge, Lincoln continues, "Respondent cares but little for said fifty dollars; if it is his legal right he prefers retaining it; but he objects to repaying it <u>once</u> to the estate of said Robert S. Todd, and <u>again</u> to said firm, or to said Petitioners; and he particularly objects to being compelled to pay money to said firm or said Petitioner's which he never received at all. Respondent prays that said Petitioners may be ruled to file a Bill of particulars, stating the <u>names</u> and <u>residences</u> of the persons of whom, they claim that Respondent has collected money belonging to them." Lincoln boldly underlined the words for emphasis.

In the cover letter, he told his attorney, "... I find it difficult to suppress my indignation towards those who have got up this claim against me ... I ask that the petitioners be ruled to file a bill of particulars ... to enable me to absolutely disprove this claim." Although he was writing to another lawyer who knew the rules as well as Lincoln, he told Kinkead anyway, "I know it is for <u>them</u> to prove their claim, rather than for <u>me</u> to disprove it; but I am unwilling to trust the oath of any man, who either <u>made</u> or <u>prompted</u> the oath to the petition." That letter shows not only Lincoln's ire, but that he also suspected that Mary's brother Levi had induced Hemmingway to bring this action in retaliation for the suit Lincoln had earlier filed against Levi.

In a July letter to Kinkead, Lincoln clearly indicates that he thinks Levi is behind the action. "In the autumn of 1849 I was at Lexington several days, during which time I was almost constantly with L.O. [Levi] Todd; and if he shall . . . think he remembers that I told him I had collected money for Oldham, Todd & Co. ...such recollection would be an utter mistake; yet if something of the sort is not relied on, I can not not [sic] conceive how Mr. Hemingway was induced to swear to the truth of the Bill...."

Through the summer and autumn, while Lincoln continued to press, through his attorney, for the "bill of particulars" which would name the names, the petitioners remained silent. Had Lincoln petitioned, the court would probably have dismissed the suit. With his honesty and integrity at risk, Mr. Lincoln was not going to let anyone off that easily.

Finally, more than five months after the case was filed, Lincoln got his names. The petitioners named Henry E. Drummer, William F. Thornton and John T. Stuart as having handed Lincoln money belonging to Oldham, Hemmingway and Todd. Within a week, Lincoln had desposed each of the named parties. Other than the $50 which Lincoln said Mr. Todd had told him to keep, each said that, while they had done business with the Kentucky firm, they had no knowledge of any money changing

hands. Typical of the information collected is Thornton's statement that he "…is certain the defendant Lincoln has never had anything to do with the collection of the note of W. F. Thornton and Basye, debtors of Oldham, Todd & Co."

When Lincoln forwarded the notarized statements to his attorney, Levi Todd (or whoever else may have been involved) gave up the ghost. On January 16, the terse comment, "Clerk of the Fayette Circuit Court will please dismiss the suit of Oldham and Todd vs. Lincoln and Edwards" appears in the court record. The note is signed, "C. D. Curr, atty for plaintiffs."

Without question, Abraham Lincoln found that result satisfying. Earlier, he had authorized his Lexington lawyer to pay himself from any funds due Lincoln which came to hand. When he received a draft for some funds Kinkead had received on his behalf, Lincoln wrote back, "I ran my eye over the contents of your letter, & only have to say you do not seem disposed to compensate yourself very liberally for the separate service you did for me" Evidently he had some sense of what an attorney's time was worth.

Lincoln's state of satisfaction and political apathy would not last long. Just over the horizon were events which, in his words "aroused him as he had never been before."

Part V

The political events which rekindled Lincoln's political interests and ambition were the Kansas-Nebraska Act and the resulting birth of the Republican Party, both of which occurred in 1854.

In March of that year Illinois Senator Stephen Douglas (Billy Herndon said "Douglas was never far away") rammed The Kansas-Nebraska Act through Congress, and President Pierce signed it into law in May. This law virtually nullified the Missouri Compromise and the Compromise of 1850. It opened the door for the spread of slavery, created Kansas and Nebraska as territories and, most importantly, under "popular sovereignty" allowed the residents of new territories to decide for themselves whether slavery would be legal in the territory. This was just too much for many of the former Whigs, who were opposed to everything Democratic, particularly the expansion of slavery. The Kansas-Nebraska

Act, which qualified on both counts, is generally credited with creating the Republican Party and recognized as the first step toward an actual shooting civil war.

Following Henry Clay's death, the Whig Party collapsed, leaving its faithful with no political home. National racism being prevalent at the time, the "Know Nothing" party was established. The name stemmed from the fact that when asked about the party organization, members were instructed to reply, "I know nothing." Not surprisingly, the organization lasted only a short while before many of the more moderate members joined the Republican Party. Many Democrats, upset by the Act, also joined Whigs in filling the ranks of the new political entity. Although more and more of the population were beginning to seek abolition of slavery, that topic was too politically charged, so the Republicans chose to try to limit slavery's growth as new territories became states. Lincoln's argument against "popular sovereignty" was "that if any one man chooses to enslave another, no third man shall be allowed to object."

Back in 1850, in a political discussion, John Stuart commented to Lincoln that "the time is coming when we shall all have to be either Abolitionists or Democrats." Lincoln thoughtfully replied, "When that time comes, my mind is made up, for I believe that the slavery question can never be successfully compromised." This is a sentiment that Mr. Lincoln would put much more eloquently in his "House Divided" speech a few years later. Lincoln no doubt disagreed with Stuart, but felt no need to tell Stuart that he wasn't about to become a Democrat and probably did not want to say he would not become an abolitionist either. Thus, Abraham Lincoln was in the forefront of the Republican Party from its inception.

As soon as the Kansas-Nebraska Act became law, Lincoln was on the stump speaking against it in the strongest of terms. So powerful were his arguments that, at one meeting, an ardent Democrat was heard to remark to no one in particular, "He's a dangerous man, sir! A damned dangerous man! He makes you believe what he says in spite of yourself." Another who heard Lincoln's stance said of the speaker, "It was evident that he had mastered his subject, knew what he was going to say and knew that he was right." Both of those comments speak well of Lincoln's speaking ability but, more importantly, to his certainty in the righteousness of his position. His

old adversary, Stephen Douglas, being the bill's sponsor, was on the other side of the argument, of course. Neither man knew it, but from this issue we can see the genesis of the famous series of Lincoln-Douglas debates. So hot was the topic and so persuasive were Lincoln's arguments that anti-Nebraska forces in surrounding states began to call upon him to speak. So, from these discussions, we can date the beginning of his national reputation.

As Illinois Congressman Richard Yates, an ardent opponent of the Kansas-Nebraska Act, was running for re-election, he became the beneficiary of some of Lincoln's oratory. Also, simply to support Yates, both Lincoln and Stephen Logan agreed to become candidates for the Illinois General Assembly. Lincoln had no interest in the State Legislature. However, he felt that a U. S. Senate seat could be had by the new party, and he planned to be the man to fill that spot currently held by his duel adversary, James Shields. Events did not play out that way; in the fall, Lincoln and Logan were elected while Yates was defeated.

Lincoln promptly resigned the General Assembly seat to which he was elected, causing a special election to choose a replacement. Freed of the Legislative responsibility, he dove headlong into the race for the Senate. At the time, Senators were chosen by the State Legislature. Because the anti-Nebraska forces had made such a good showing in the general elections, Lincoln felt that the Senate seat was within his grasp. That was not to be, either. Backroom politics caused the slot to go to anti-Nebraska Democrat Lyman Trumbull.

Lincoln's disappointment over the Senate loss, his stance on current issues and his hope for the future are evident in a letter to Joshua Speed written on August 24, 1855. He begins by saying that he supposes he and his Kentucky friend disagree on slavery. "You know I dislike slavery, and you fully admit the abstract wrong of it." Lincoln says, however, that he is not asking Speed (or anyone) to yield the right to hold slaves, although "I confess that I hate to see the poor creatures hunted down ... but I bite my lip and keep quiet." Lincoln reveals that he understands the political implications of his position with "You say that if

Lincoln's friend and arch-rival Senator Stephen A. Douglas.

Kansas fairly votes herself a free State, as a Christian, you will rejoice at it. All decent slaveholders talk that way, and I do not doubt their candor. But they never vote that way. Although in a private letter or conversation you will express your preference that Kansas shall be free, you would vote for no man for Congress who would say the same thing publicly." That sentence seems to make clear that he still has his eye on the United States Senate.

Sometime in December, "Little Sister," Emilie Todd came to visit Mary Lincoln and her other Springfield relatives. The prettiest of the Todd girls, the sprightly nineteen-year-old was as much of an asset to Springfield's

winter society as her older sisters had been in their day. For the rest of her long and eventful life, Emilie would remember the good times she had shared with the Lincolns. When she went home, she became the only one of the Todd girls to return to Lexington unmarried.

In January 1855, Lincoln bought a notebook in which he listed all the members of the Illinois legislature (who would elect the next Senator) classifying each as D (Democrat), W (Whig) or A.N.D (Anti-Nebraska Democrat.) The tally is 41 D, 37 W and 19 A.N.D. Surely, he calculated that the AND's would join the W's in becoming Republicans, so he figured the count at 41 Democrats vs. 56 Republicans. If that worked out, his chances for the Senate looked very good. Even though the Senatorial campaign was two years away, just to nudge the members along, Lincoln hosted a dinner for all the Anti-Nebraska legislators on February 15.

Biding his time working behind the scenes and on his law cases, Lincoln held out until the Kansas-Nebraska Act had created so much turmoil that a convention of all Anti-Nebraska men was called to meet in Bloomington in May 1856. This meeting, attended by former Whigs, Anti-Nebraska Democrats and those who just disliked Stephen Douglas, marks the birth of the Republican Party – sometimes referred to as the "Free-Soil" party – in Illinois. In the course of the meeting, they nominated candidates for state offices and adopted a strong anti-popular sovereignty platform. Before adjournment, the delegates called upon Mr. Lincoln to make a "keynote" address. His hour-and-a-half speech so mesmerized the crowd that even the meticulous Herndon failed to take notes. As no transcript exists, this is Lincoln's "Lost Speech," but Herndon records that in denouncing the spread of slavery, his partner, "had the fever of a new convert … his eyes were aglow with an inspiration ….His speech was full of fire and energy and force; it was logic, it was pathos, it was justice, equity, truth and light….If Mr. Lincoln was six feet, four inches high usually, at Bloomington that day, he was seven feet…. From that day until his death, he stood firmly in the right." The fledgling Republican Party had found its leader.

Evidence of Lincoln's prominence was provided at the Republican national convention held in Philadelphia two weeks later. Lincoln, unable to attend because of an extra session of the Champaign Circuit Court, nonetheless kept a close watch on the proceedings as John C. Freemont, "The Pathfinder," was nominated for President by a small margin over New York's William Seward. Considering the Vice Presidential nominee, the Chicago paper reported the vote: "Dayton 259, Lincoln 110, Ford 7 …" before a gentleman from Massachusetts withdrew several of the lower vote-count candidates. On the final vote, Dayton received the nomination, with Lincoln running a close second. Herndon and other friends were elated at the national recognition their man was receiving, but Lincoln, as usual, downplayed the incident. "I reckon that ain't me," he remarked, "there's another great man in Massachusetts named Lincoln, and I reckon it's him."

Democratic candidate James Buchanan warned that electing a "black" Republican would lead to Civil War, while ex-president Millard Fillmore, the Know Nothing entry, ignored the popular sovereignty issue in favor of denouncing existing immigration policies. Despite Lincoln's all-out efforts on behalf of the new Party, on election day the public endorsed Douglas' extension of slavery by electing Buchanan albeit by the margin of only 50,000 votes out of the nearly 4 million cast. In a clear picture of sectional strife, nearly all of The Pathfinder's votes came from Northern States, while the already fairly "Solid South" put the Democratic man in the White House. As a boon to the new political party, the Republican William H. Bissell, was elected Governor of Illinois on the same day.

Lincoln had predicted the outcome, although he perhaps did not anticipate the muscle his Party would flex on the first time out. When he told a reporter that a Republican President would be elected sooner or later, the journalist asked, "Do you think we shall elect a Free-Soil President in 1860?"

Lincoln replied that he, of course, didn't know, but, "As I said before, the Free-Soil Party is bound to win in the long run." If he even dreamed that he would be the man to carry the banner, he gave no hint.

Although deeply involved in the politics, Mr. Lincoln still had a law practice. One of his best known cases, defending the Illinois Central Railroad (ICRR) was going on coincident with the political action. This case explodes the myth that Lincoln never sued to collect a fee.

Early in 1853, when the ICRR was chartered, the

The actual stove on which Mary Todd Lincoln prepared the family meals.

railroad agreed to give 5% of its gross profits to the State in return for which all ICRR property would be exempt from taxes for six years. Soon after the ICRR began operations, McLean County filed a suit to force the ICRR to pay County taxes, an obligation the ICRR felt they could not meet. Mr. Lincoln was paid a retainer of $250 to represent the ICRR. When the case was called in the fall of 1854, Lincoln lost the argument when the court ruled against the railroad.

An appeal was taken to the Supreme Court where the case was re-argued in February 1855. The opposing attorneys were, interestingly enough, Lincoln's former partners, Logan and Stuart. The case was continued and did not come up again until January 1856. This time, Lincoln won the argument; the lower court ruling was reversed and the ICRR did not have to pay county taxes.

> *"As I said before, the Free-Soil Party is bound to win in the long run."*
>
> –Lincoln

Here the stories differ a bit, but Herndon's version seems the most likely. According to his partner, Lincoln personally went to Chicago where he submitted a bill for $2000 to a company official, who Herndon says may have been none other than ICRR Superintendent George B. McClellan, who, in a few years, would deal President Lincoln plenty of misery as the reticent commander of the Union Army. At any rate, the ICRR said the fee was excessive and refused to pay as it was "as much as Daniel Webster himself would charge." On the way home, Lincoln met some attorney friends who opined that the $2000 fee was too modest and encouraged him to increase his demand from the ICRR to $5000. Evidently Lincoln agreed; he filed suit for his $5000 fee.

An official of the ICRR met with Lincoln. If an offer to settle was made, Lincoln refused, stating the strength of his position. Although Herndon does not mention the fact, the railroad officials were certainly aware that Lincoln was a powerful Illinois politician and, as such, was in a position to do the ICRR (always a political animal) a good deal of good or harm if he so chose.

The case was called in McLean County Court in June 1857. As no attorney appeared on behalf of the company, a judgment for $5000 went to Lincoln by default. When an ICRR attorney did appear that afternoon, the court granted his request that the judgment be set aside, so the case was re-scheduled. At that hearing, the court ruled that the $5000 fee was reasonable and ordered the company to pay up. After a month, still not having received his money, Lincoln had the sheriff impound enough of the ICRR's property to satisfy the judgment. With that, the ICRR saw the wisdom of paying the fee. When the financial panic of 1857 struck the country's economy soon after, Lincoln and Herndon "thanked the Lord for letting the Illinois Central fall into our hands."

Another case that deserves attention took place in the summer of 1857 in Cincinnati. Cyrus McCormick was suing a man named Manny for patent infringement on his mechanical reaper. Only after Lincoln agreed to represent Manny, did he learn – to his dismay – that famous Ohio lawyer, Edwin Stanton had subsequently been retained as co-counsel. The details of the case are unimportant; it is only worth mention because Mr. Stanton continuously insulted Mr. Lincoln throughout the trial, usurping the lead counsel role even though Lincoln, being retained first, was entitled to that honor. Back in Springfield, Lincoln told Herndon that through an open door he had heard Stanton ask someone "Where did that long-armed creature come from and what does he expect to accomplish in this case?" Lincoln would remember his "rough treatment" at Stanton's hands when they met again in Washington in 1861.

Perhaps Lincoln's best known case, made so partly by John Ford's 1939 (what a great year for movies!) movie *Young Mr. Lincoln*, was an outstanding defense of William "Duff" Armstrong, son of Lincoln's New Salem wrestling adversary and Black Hawk War friend, the now dead Jack Armstrong. At an August 29, 1857 camp meeting, Duff and James Norris allegedly conspired to kill a man. Another jury had already convicted Norris when Armstrong came to trial in the spring of 1858. Lincoln was eager to defend his old friend's son, assuring Hanna, Duff's mother, that her boy would be acquitted. Due to the entertainment value of a murder trial and Mr. Lincoln's political prominence, the Beardstown courtroom was packed as the opening statements began.

The prosecution's star witness was Charles Allen who had already help convict Armstrong's alledged conspirator

by testifying that in the bright moonlight on that August night, he had seen Norris hit the victim on the head with a club and then observed Armstrong strike another blow. Lounging in his chair, Lincoln apparently paid no heed to Allen's testimony.

On cross-examination, Lincoln casually asked a few irrelevant questions and then had Allen repeat what he had seen. Warming to the task, Lincoln asked Allen how far away he was from the action. Told it was about 150 feet, Lincoln then asked what time the fight occurred. After Allen said about 11 PM, and said he could see from that distance at that time because the full moon was high in the sky and bright as daylight, Lincoln shed all appearances of nonchalance as he asked the sheriff to bring in the 1857 almanac. Turning to August, the lawyer had the witness read that the moon on the night of the 29th was barely past the first quarter and had set by 11 PM.

Despite his having totally discredited the eye-witness testimony, Lincoln's case was not yet won. The prosecution strove mightily to recover. On defense Lincoln called a doctor who testified that the first blow could well have killed the dead man and several others attesting to Armstrong's character.

Then, closing arguments. The prosecutor reviewed his case, skirting Allen testimony and closing by pleaded with the jury to convict Armstrong of the "atrocious crime" to set an example for other young men.

Lincoln stood and rose to heights of eloquence rare even for him. He reviewed the evidence, hammering every weak point, then demonstrated, from an astounding knowledge of anatomy, that the first blow was most likely fatal. Another lawyer, sitting in the gallery, said that as Lincoln spoke, "his eyes brightened perceptibly, and every facial movement seemed to emphasize his feeling and add expression to his thoughts" as he told the jury how Hanna and Jack Armstrong had taken him in when he was a penniless youth in New Salem. Tears – genuine, insists the prosecutor – streamed down the lawyer's cheeks as he informed the jury that he was defending Duff not for a fee, but rather to prevent the hopelessness, poverty, misery and suffering that would befall the poor widow should they convict Duff. A suspender fell unnoticed from his shoulder as he closed by saying that God had given him the opportunity to repay Hanna for her kindness to him

and he prayed he'd be worthy of the chore. As Lincoln sat, several of the hard-working jury men were seen to wipe tears from their eyes with calloused hands. Duff was acquitted on the first jury ballot.

"I have said a hundred times," moaned the prosecutor years later, "it was Lincoln's speech that saved that criminal from the gallows."

Part VI

The Illinois Senatorial term for the seat occupied by Stephen Douglas was to expire in 1858. Mr. Douglas, one of the most powerful men in the Senate, intended, of course, to be re-elected and retain his seat. Mr. Lincoln intended replace him, thus becoming the first Illinois Republican to sit in the United States Senate.

In April, the Democrats officially made Douglas their candidate. In June, the Republicans showed their optimism by announcing "That Hon. Abraham Lincoln is our first and only choice for United States Senator to fill the vacancy about to be created by the expiration of Mr. Douglas' term of office."

Lincoln expected the nomination; indeed had worked and planned on it for nearly 18 months. Long before the announcement, he was composing his acceptance speech, which as it turns out, would become one of the greatest of his career. In that speech, delivered in the House Chamber of the Illinois Capitol and against the counsel of those around him, he made his political testament clear: "A house divided against itself cannot stand. I believe this government cannot endure, permanently half slave and half free. I do not expect the Union to be dissolved — I do not expect the house to fall — but I do expect it will cease to be divided.

"It will become all one thing or all the other. Either the opponents of slavery will arrest the further spread of it, and

> *"A house divided against itself cannot stand. I believe this government cannot endure, permanently half slave and half free. I do not expect the Union to be dissolved — I do not expect the house to fall — but I do expect it will cease to be divided.*
> *–Lincoln*

In Representatives Hall of the old capitol, Lincoln sat in the Legislature and gave his "House Divided" speech. The Lincoln style hat marks where he sat as a Sate Legislator.

place it where the public mind shall rest in the belief that it is in the course of ultimate extinction; or its advocates will push it forward, 'til it shall become alike lawful in all the States, old as well as new — North as well as South."

Herndon and the other Republicans warned that this language was entirely too strong – that this wording, even if an accurate reflection of his political goals, would never get him elected. Lincoln said that now was the time for action on the slavery question – the issue had been skirted for long enough. His comment, "If it is decreed that I should go down because of this speech, then let me go down linked to the truth" reflects the "what will be, will be," philosophy Mrs. Lincoln said was her husband's creed.

With the campaign issue clearly defined, the battle was joined. As we have seen, Lincoln, at age 49, was by now a veteran campaigner – strong on the stump, quick with the facts and tempered against the strongest rivals, including Stephen Douglas. In fact, Douglas had admitted that he had never faced a more formidable debater than Lincoln, even in Congress.

Stephen Douglas, on the other hand, was no pushover. Illinois Senator since 1847 with a strong local career before that, Douglas, age 45, was a seasoned politician. At just over five feet tall, he had worked hard to earn the sobriquet "Little Giant." His assessment of Lincoln's speaking skill is impressive in that Douglas had crossed verbal swords with the likes of Henry Clay, Andrew Jackson, William Seward and Daniel Webster among many others. Early in his career he was friendly and open with all, but by 1858 Douglas had polished his manners and mien to match his resume – a consummate man of the world.

Lincoln and Douglas were as unlike in their political allegiances as they were physically opposite. Lincoln had marked his ground with the "house divided" speech; Douglas stood firm on the principle of popular sovereignty. Still, even political opponents can respect each other; these two faced off as old friends and foes. Both men relished

Knox College's Old Main at Galesburg, IL is the only Lincoln-Douglas debate site still standing.

The plaques flanking the door honor the two men who spoke from a platform constructed on this end of the building.

The building at Knox College in Galesburg, Illinois where the Lincoln-Douglas Debate took place as it was circa 1864, only a few years after the famous event. Courtesy of Knox College Public Relations.

this opportunity to test themselves and their political beliefs before the public. Senator Douglas, of course, already enjoyed a wide public reputation, but this campaign, being of countrywide interest, would bring Abraham Lincoln to the nation's attention.

Douglas opened his campaign with a speech in Chicago on July 9. The speaker delivered a masterful indictment of his opponent who stood quietly in the audience. The next evening Lincoln responded from the same venue. Lincoln denied Douglas' charge that he was an abolitionist,

although declaring that he hated slavery as much as any one of them, but went further with "I should like to know if taking this old Declaration of Independence, which declares that all men are equal upon principle and making exceptions to it, where will it stop. If one man says it does not mean a negro, why not another say it does not mean some other man?"

Over the next three weeks, Lincoln heard Douglas speak several times. At each meeting, when the crowd called for him to answer, Lincoln begged off, saying that as the meeting was called by Douglas' friends, for him to speak would be improper. Perhaps the germ of the idea come from those calls to respond, but on July 24th, at the urging of his advisors, Lincoln challenged his opponent to a series of joint debates, one in each of the seven congressional districts where neither had yet spoken. Four days later, the two men dined together, leaving no record of what was discussed, other than the fact that the debate proposal did not come up. Before returning to his office that evening, Lincoln read in the paper that Douglas had accepted his challenge, and, upon arrival, he found the letter of acceptance which also suggested sites and terms for the meetings. After some discussion, Lincoln accepted his opponent's terms, even though "you take four openings and closes to my three." As there were an odd number of meetings, obviously somebody had to take three; evidently Abe just wanted to keep the record straight.

"If it is decreed that I should go down because of this speech, then let me go down linked to the truth"

–Lincoln

Douglas' agenda called for meeting at Ottawa on August 21, Freeport August 27, Jonesboro September 15, Charleston September 18, Galesburg October 7, Qunicy October 13 and Alton October 15. Unfortunately for us, only at Galesburg where the two candidates met at Knox College's "Old Main" can we find the only debate site still in existence. A huge crowd – perhaps the largest on any of the debates showed up despite the raw, blustery late-fall weather. To help combat a cold west wind, a last-minute decision was made to hold the speaking on the east side of the building. In their haste to erect a speaker's platform on that end, workers managed to construct it blocking the door. Hence, the speakers had to enter through the front

door, walk down the hall and crawl through a window onto the platform. When he did so, Abe Lincoln was heard to remark, "Well, I've been through college now." The "Lincoln Window," to the left of the door, is now in the Knox College President's office.

Typical as that comment is of his jovial attitude between debates and on the road, in the contests, Lincoln was all business. All the sites were near Illinois' border, so the crowds were swelled by adjoining states' residents. In front of huge crowds and the national newspaper media at each venue, he certainly attacked his opponent, but, just as he managed in the courtroom, he did so without rancor. Throughout the debates, Douglas charged that Lincoln personally was an abolitionist, that the "Black Republicans" intended to outlaw slavery and hence dissolve the Union and grant Negro citizenship and suffrage. Lincoln consistently denied these allegations, pointing out that he was merely applying the Constitution with statements such as "I do not understand that just because I do not want a Negro woman for a slave I necessarily want her for a wife." He emphasized that the equality he was interested in was a matter of Jefferson's "inalienable rights," not restricted by size or color and reiterated that he had no intent to interfere with slavery where it already existed.

Political parties and candidates always try to appear to have different stances, even when they do not significantly disagree. In truth, Douglas' ideas were not all that different from Lincoln's as neither man had in mind any marked change in the "peculiar institution" as slavery was usually referred to in those days. Both men, no doubt, realized that issues larger than an Illinois Senate seat were being contested. While Douglas knew that, even though Southern Democrats had no dog in this fight, his reelection was imperative to the slaveholders who wanted him in Congress. He also knew that careful wording would be required to avoid offending his Southern supporters. The 1860 Presidential campaign was not far away and he'd need those Democrat votes to put him in the White House.

Lincoln, determined to eventually see a Republican elected as president, hoped to force Douglas to defend his non-slaveholding supporters at the expense of pro-slavery Democrats. If Douglas did that, Southern Democrats would think he'd waffled on the issue. Accordingly, at Freeport on

Modern visitors to Lincoln's home are allowed to utilize the original walnut stair rail.

August 27, Lincoln answered the questions his opponent had posed to him in the first meeting at Ottawa six days earlier and then, again against advice of other Republicans, hit Douglas with, "Can the people of a United States Territory, in any lawful way, against the wish of any citizen of the United States, exclude slavery from its limits prior to the formation of a State constitution?" Lincoln was certain that Douglas would say that it was possible to exclude slavery from a territory and that when he did, he'd forfeit Southern Democrats' support for President.

When his turn to speak came, Douglas unhesitatingly responded, saying, "...a majority of the people thereof [a territory] have the lawful means to introduce or exclude it [slavery] as they please.... Hence, no matter what the decisions of the Supreme Court may be on that abstract question, still the right of the people to make a slave territory or a free territory is perfect and complete under the Nebraska bill." The Democrats in attendance that evening wildly cheered their approval of that response, evidently

not realizing the national implications. If Stephen Douglas was aware, he perhaps thought that after he was reelected, he'd have time to mend his national fences but, his answer would soon precipitate a deep split in the Democratic Party. That schism would be a major factor in Lincoln's 1860 election and another step on the road to civil war.

On a cold rainy November 2, 1858, the people of Illinois went to the polls to make their will known by electing the Legislators who would choose the Senator. Despite receiving less than half the votes, the apportionment of the districts put a Democratic majority in the General Assembly.

In January 1859, in joint session, the Illinois Legislature partisan nominations proposed Stephen Douglas and Abraham Lincoln for Senator. When the roll call was finished, Stephen Douglas was re-elected by a vote of 54-46. A disappointed Lincoln told a reporter that he felt like the boy who had stubbed his toe. "I'm too big to cry, but it hurts too bad to laugh."

With his usual foresight, Lincoln wrote a (non-political) friend, " I am glad I made the late race. It gave me a hearing on the great and durable question of the age which I could have had in no other way: and though I now sink out of view and shall be forgotten, I believe I have made some marks which will tell for the cause of civil liberty long after I am gone."

He might not have been laughing; indeed, his prospects may have looked bleak at that moment. His comments indicate that he clearly did not think he had much of a future in politics. The "marks " he had made may have been satisfying, but Abraham Lincoln went home after the Senatorial contest reveling in the secure knowledge that Stephen Douglas – the Democrat's most formidable candidate – would never be President. He would work – as he always had – to support his party and attempt to ensure the election of a Republican in 1860, no matter who carried the banner.

Part VII

Having paid most of his campaign expenses out of his own pocket, when the canvass ended, Abraham Lincoln needed to earn some money. Hence, he turned his focus back to his long-neglected law practice.

He did help out his partner with the legal work, but

In this parlor at his home, Abe received the Republican committee that informed him that he had been nominated for President in 1860.

politics would not stay out of his mind for long. The debates with Douglas had gained him enough of a regional reputation that requests to speak on the Party's behalf in surrounding states holding elections began to filter into the Springfield office. With an eye to the upcoming Presidential election, Lincoln's name was mentioned as a candidate locally, but New York's former Senator William Seward, was the nominal leader of the party and Ohio's Salmon P. Chase had his backers, too.

On September 17, 1859, Abe, Mary and Tad left Springfield bound for an engagement in Ohio. En route, between trains in Dayton, he made an impromptu address, speaking to a crowd in Hamilton. That evening in Cincinnati, knowing there were many slave-owning Kentuckians in the crowd, he reiterated the Republican position. "We mean to treat you, as nearly as we can, like Washington, Jefferson and Madison treated you. We mean to leave you alone…."

Striking similar notes in speeches in Kansas, Wisconsin and Indiana, Lincoln must have been somewhat taken aback

when an invitation to speak at well-known anti-slavery minister Henry Ward Beecher's church in Brooklyn, New York arrived at his office. The offer was from anti-Seward Republicans including Horace Greeley and William Cullen Bryan. He was probably also delighted as the offer included expenses and a $200 stipend. Well aware that radical Southerners had threatened to secede if a Republican was elected President, he accepted the offer and scheduled his talk for late February 1860.

By the time Lincoln arrived in New York, so many people were demanding tickets that his meeting had been moved to the Cooper Institute.

Lincoln began by quoting (from a newspaper) Stephen Douglas' remark that "Our fathers, when they framed the Government under which we live, understood this question just as well, and even better, than we do now." In total agreement with that sentiment, he proceeded to examine – backed by an impressive volume of preparatory research – the views of the 39 signers of the Constitution. Lincoln observed that a majority of them believed Congress should

Congressman Abraham Lincoln in 1846. Library of Congress

When Lincoln went to Congress in 1846, he and his wife had their portraits made. Mary Todd Lincoln had two children by the time this shot was taken. Library of Congress

108

In the Governor's office in the old Illinois Capitol, President-elect Lincoln received hordes of job seekers.

control slavery in the territories, making no provision for its expansion. Clearly, he said, the current Republican policy was neither new nor revolutionary, and should not alarm Southerners

As was usual when Lincoln spoke to an unfamiliar audience, they were first struck by his clumsy appearance, but were quickly won over by what he said. An eyewitness gave testimony: "When Lincoln rose to speak, I was greatly disappointed. He was tall, tall, – oh, how tall! and so angular and awkward that I had, for an instant, a feeling of pity for so ungainly a man." However, once Lincoln warmed up, "his face lighted up as with an inward fire; the whole man was transfigured. I forgot his clothes, his personal appearance, and his individual peculiarities. Presently, forgetting myself, I was on my feet like the rest, yelling like a wild Indian, cheering this wonderful man."

This speech is clearly one of Lincoln best efforts, thoroughly researched, beautifully crafted and brilliantly delivered. He effectively attacked the Democrats' policy,

defended the Republicans' and made a striking impression for himself in Seward's home territory.

Leaving New York, he decided to work in a visit with son Bob, then a student at Philips Exeter Academy in Exeter, New Hampshire in preparation for Harvard. Lincoln spoke at various locations in Connecticut and Rhode Island as well as New Hampshire, everywhere eliciting the same reaction as in New York. This report is typical: "For the first half-hour, his opponents would agree with every word he uttered; and from that point he would lead them off, little by little, until it seemed as if he had got them all into the fold."

Herndon says that the popular idea that his partner stood by doing nothing while popular passion and destiny swept Lincoln into the Presidency is undiluted myth. Lincoln wanted the nomination, felt that it was within his grasp, worked diligently to gain it and understated the case when he told a friend, "The taste is in my mouth a little."

In May 1860, the Republican State Convention

was held at Decatur. When John Hanks brought in the aforementioned rails and the chairman declared that they were symbolic of the contest between free labor (Republicans) and slave labor (Democrats,) Lincoln was a shoo-in to secure the vote of the Illinois delegation at the national convention meeting in Chicago a week later. Lincoln was delighted that Hanks, a life-long Democrat, had swapped allegiances.

At the huge wooden "Wigwam" in Chicago, after the first two days were consumed building a Party platform, Lincoln's name was very much before the convention, as was Seward's. At home in Springfield, – Lincoln worked behind the scenes having told his representatives that he had no desire to make a public statement on any subject, he would not accept the Vice Presidential nomination and to "make no contracts which will bind me." Knowing that their man would get no votes from the South, the delegates felt that the nominee would have to not only embody the

These marbles are displayed in the Lincoln boys' bedroom.

Party's principles, but also be conservative enough to carry the "border" states. In Kentucky, Maryland, Delaware and Missouri, slavery was legal, but Union sentiment generally prevailed. Note, in passing, that West Virginia also fell into that category, but did not exist as a separate entity until 1863. Although many felt that Seward could not hold the border states, he garnered a smaller-than-expected lead on the first ballot, Lincoln trailing by a count of 173 ½ to 102. Chase was far down the list and fading. By the second ballot Chase disappeared, his votes going to Lincoln. Also, many New England voters – Seward's supposed strength – switched. These changes narrowed the gap to a mere 3½ votes.

At this juncture, Addison G. Proctor, the youngest member of the Kansas delegation, comes into play. Having a delegation from a territory was unusual, but the Party felt that as "Bleeding Kansas" had suffered so much and was at the root of the issue, they were invited to attend as voting members. When the decision to allow Kansas votes was challenged, none other than William Seward came to the defense. Addison said that on the evening of the second day, the Kansas delegation received word that " a committee of border state Unionists" would like to confer with them. When the room was filled, "their spokesman stepped forward." According to Proctor, this man was Kentucky's redoubtable emancipationist, Cassius M. Clay. Proctor goes on to say that Clay warned that there were those determined to dissolve the Union and such would be the case unless the convention named "a leader who will inspire our confidence and our courage."

Addison concludes, "Leaning forward in a half-suppressed whisper, he [Clay] said, 'we want you to name Abraham Lincoln.'" In his memoirs, Clay himself says that although he was a Lincoln supporter, "I did not go to the convention." Addison related his story several times before his death in 1925, so evidently he thought Clay was there. If both men are right, Addison misidentified the speaker.

However it happened, in the middle of the third ballot, Mr. Carter of Ohio stood on his chair shouting to be recognized. "I rise, Mr. Chairman," he yelled, "to announce the change of four votes of Ohio from Mr. Chase to Mr. Lincoln." The rout was on, Lincoln swept to victory. For a running mate, Cassius Clay received 101

As the Republican Party had never before offered a Presidential slate, this 1860 campaign poster provided much information about the party's platform as well as pictures of candidates Lincoln and Hannibal Hamlin. Hardin County Museum

votes on the initial count, but the slot went "for geographic purposes" to Maine's Hannibal Hamlin. Clay, "The Lion of White Hall," says, "If I had been there, I could have had the Vice-Presidential nomination over anyone."

Lincoln, who had been hanging around trying to give the appearance that all was as usual, was waiting at the newspaper office back in Springfield, where the word came quickly. Handed the telegram, he said, "Well, gentlemen, there is a little short woman at our house who is probably more interested in this dispatch than I am; if you will excuse me, I will take it up and let her see it." If he indeed said that, it may have been Lincoln's attempt at a little humor, but that comment may be the basis of some of the speculation that she pushed him into public office.

Formal notice of his nomination came the next day, May 19, when a notification committee arrived in Springfield in late afternoon, and called at Lincoln's Eighth Street home at 8 PM. When they arrived, a dozen or so Springfield residents were waiting outside and one

of the Lincoln boys was swinging on the gatepost. He received them in the north parlor (on the left of the hall), and responded briefly to the address of the convention chairman, George Ashmun of Massachusetts. Shaking hands with Mr. Kelly of Pennsylvania, Lincoln asked how tall Kelly was. Informed that the gentleman was six-feet-three, Lincoln said, "I beat you, I am six-feet-four without boots."

"I am glad," responded Kelly, "that we have found a candidate we can all look up to as we had been informed that there were only little giants in Illinois."

The entire group then moved across the hall, to south parlor, where the members were presented to Mrs. Lincoln and treated to ice water, the strongest drink allowed in the house. One wonders how Willie and Tad were kept out of the way.

At about the same time as the Republicans were pow-wowing at the Wigwam, the Democratic Convention met in Charleston, South Carolina. The leading candidate,

Campaign advertisement for Lincoln - Hamlin. Hardin County Museum

Stephen Douglas, would now pay the piper for his reply to Lincoln's Freeport question. Feeling that Douglas had wavered in his support of slavery, the southern wing of the party demanded the adoption of a platform which explicitly protected the institution. When the north refused to acquiesce, an Alabama delegate announced that, "We came here with one great purpose, to save our Constitutional rights." It was not the last time that phrase would be heard over the next five years. With that, the Southern states' delegates stormed out leaving less than the two-thirds majority necessary to nominate any candidate.

When they re-convened in Baltimore in June, turf battles, indicative of the deep rift in the Party, erupted over which delegates were certificated as some who had walked out in Charleston were in attendance while others had been replaced. When the dust settled, the convention nominated, as expected, Stephen Douglas on his popular sovereignty platform. "Southern" Democrats, meeting across town and pledged to preserve slavery, nominated Kentucky's John C. Breckenridge, currently President Buchanan's Vice President, while yet a third faction, the "Constitutional Union" Democrats put Tennessee's John Bell in the race, their platform being to ignore the slavery question altogether.

While it would not be fair to say that Lincoln did not campaign, it is a fact that he made no speech, as was usual in those days. As the legislature was on recess, the Governor made his room in the State House available for Lincoln's use, and John Nicolay was appointed to help with the correspondence. He did see anyone who came to interview him and answer any questions he was asked, as long as it was not political, wrote letters and encouraged the Party faithful, but he let others go on the stump. If you're tired of television ads for political candidates, you have Stephen Douglas to thank – he broke with tradition and was thus the first to ever actively campaign for himself for President.

Among the correspondence was a letter which proves yet another Lincoln story. In a letter, Grace Bedell, an 11 year-old New Yorker, asked about Mr. Lincoln's children and suggested that his appearance might be improved by a beard. In answer, to the "Dear Little Miss" on October 19, he told her he had only sons and wrote, "...As to the whiskers, I have never worn any, do you not think that people would call it a silly piece of affectation were I to begin wearing them now?"

Evidently he agreed with her about the beard. Grace reported that when the President-elect's train stopped in her home town, Westfield, Lincoln asked that she be brought to the station. He said, "you see that I have let these whiskers grow for you." For the rest of her life, Grace would remember that Lincoln kissed her and shook her hand before departing.

Being a major party's candidate for President made little difference in Mr. Lincoln's daily routine. Approached by a stranger on the street, Abe was asked for directions to the State House. "I'm going there myself," he replied, "come along." The stranger was astounded when his guide walked around the desk in the Governor's office and announced, "I'm Lincoln, what can I do for you?"

One of the letters he wrote was to Hannibal Hamlin, the Vice Presidential candidate. They had been in the Congress simultaneously, but Lincoln did not remember having met his running mate. So, "It appears to me that you and I ought to be acquainted ...." Almost pleadingly, he added, "I shall be pleased to receive a line from you," and closed with the optimism he felt, "The prospect of Republican success now appears very flattering."

Election day was November 6, 1860 and proved Lincoln's optimism well founded. Some 4.5 million American men went to the polls, casting almost 2 million votes for Lincoln, a little less than 1.5 million for Douglas, 850,000 for Breckenridge and 600,000 for Bell. As interesting as those numbers are, the distribution of states is even more interesting. Lincoln, who was not even on the ballot in the Southern states, carried all the Northern states and California and Oregon. As Seward was rejected because it was felt he could not carry the "border" states, it is interesting that those states are not in that list: Kentucky went to Bell, despite its

An original 1864 Presidential campaign ribbon displays the sentiments of the National Union Party on which Lincoln and Andrew Johnson ran. The tintype photograph of Lincoln featured on this ribbon is the same portrait used for the $5 bill. Hardin County Museum

being John C. Breckenridge's and Mary Lincoln's home, Maryland and Delaware went to Breckenridge, and Missouri was the only state Douglas carried.

As Vice President, the chore of overseeing the tallying of electoral votes fell to John C. Breckenridge. On February 13, 1861, when Congress met in joint session for that purpose, rumors were rife on Capitol Hill, including one that Breckenridge would refuse to make the announcement should Lincoln win. Anyone who thought that did not understand that gentleman's character. Most of those present carried a concealed pistol just in case trouble should erupt. Breckenridge, probably armed himself, maintained order as each envelope was opened

giving no outward sign of emotion as votes mounted for Lincoln and himself. Finally, he rose to his full height. After a slight pause, he cleared his throat and in a ringing voice announced, "Abraham Lincoln, having received a majority of the whole number of electoral votes, is duly elected president of the United States for the four year term beginning March 4, 1861."

The electoral vote – based on the votes in congressional districts within the states – was not even close: Lincoln 180, Breckenridge 72, Bell 39 and Douglas 12.

Abe Lincoln, the backwoods rail-splitter, would be the first Republican to occupy the White House.

Part VIII

Patronage. It's the grease that makes the wheels of politics go 'round – another of the things that does not change about our system of government. What is true about job-seekers and political appointments today was equally true – if not more so – in 1860.

Being the President-elect made a huge difference in Abraham Lincoln's daily routine. As the Republican Party had only been in existence since 1856, and obviously never been in the White House before, every Democratic office holder expected to be thrown out and every Republican applicant expected to be granted some government post. The office seekers flocked to the Illinois State House to beseech the President-elect, who felt obligated to see every one. Lincoln made no promises, however. He told each one a story and gave the impression that he'd seriously consider the request, whatever it was, even if he didn't remember until the supplicant was out the door. He also left each feeling that he was free to choose whoever he liked for all posts. So many and persistent were the petitioners that even before he left for Washington, Abe told Herndon that he was tired of being President already. That attitude would be greatly enhanced. During the war, president Lincoln commented "If to be the head of Hell is as hard as what I have to undergo here, I could find it in my heart to pity Satan himself."

One of the stories surviving from those meetings is of a delegation that urged Lincoln to appoint their favorite as commissioner to the Sandwich Islands. Not only was he immensely competent they assured, but in such poor

health that the favorable climate would be good for him. With a sigh, Lincoln said, "I regret to inform you that I've already had eight applicants for that position and they are all sicker than your man."

Until he left for Washington, despite constant urgings and attempts to get a commitment of some kind on the gathering crisis, Mr. Lincoln refused to say anything concerning policy other than he believed that the government had no Constitutional right to interfere with slavery where it existed and that the Constitution also provided slave owners protection of their property.

Patronage promises had, of course, been made. Herndon says outright that cabinet posts had been promised to Simon Cameron and Caleb Smith and probably others. The former was a wealthy former Know-Nothing from Pennsylvania who became Secretary of War and the latter was appointed Secretary of the Interior upon little qualification aside from the fact that he was the man who seconded Lincoln's nomination at the Chicago Convention. Both of these men proved quite ineffective as Secretaries and were soon replaced, lending credence to Herndon's assertion. Almost everyone Lincoln chose for his cabinet had been a rival for the Republican nomination and so, it proved to be an inharmonious group until the firm hand of President Lincoln set each of them straight in their respective roles. Evidently Lincoln had made his Cabinet choices before he left for Washington.

Two weeks after the election, Lincoln made arrangements to meet Hannibal Hamlin in Chicago to discuss the cabinet personnel. On November 19, he wrote his old friend Joshua Speed requesting that he and "Mrs. S." meet him and Mary there. The two future executives did meet and, no doubt, laid out the cabinet appointments (Hamblin would do little else in his term as Vice-president.) While Fanny Speed and Mary Lincoln were shopping, Lincoln indicated that he would offer his old friend almost any job he wanted. Addressing his old pal as "Mr. President," Speed declined saying that "I do not think that you have

> *"I regret to inform you that I've already had eight applicants for that position and they are all sicker than your man."*
> —Lincoln

Abraham Lincoln. Library of Congress

within your gift any office I could afford to take." Lincoln told Speed that he wanted to appoint James Guthrie, a Louisville politician who had served President Franklin Pierce as Secretary of the Treasury, as Secretary of War, and asked Speed to make the offer in person. Speed did, Guthrie declined and, as noted, Smith went into the Cabinet.

One day in this period, Abe happened to meet an old New Salem friend, Isaac Cogsdale on the street. In 1865 Cogsdale told Herndon that Lincoln asked him to call at the State House late that afternoon, which he did. After the two talked over old times and Lincoln had inquired about all the New Salem folks, Cogsdale asked permission to ask Lincoln a question. Given the go-ahead, Cogsdale asked about Ann Rutledge. He told Herndon that Lincoln said, "I loved the woman dearly … she was a handsome girl and would have made a good loving wife…. I did honestly and truly love the girl and think often of her now." That's almost as if Herndon knew in 1865 of the criticism he would receive when his book was finally published 30 years later.

Despite the excitement, the gathering storm clouds were always overhead. On December 20, South Carolina was the first state to declare her intention to withdraw from the Union. Then, a few days before Christmas, the President-elect was informed of a rumor that President Buchanan had instructed Major Anderson to surrender Fort Sumter if attacked, Lincoln exclaimed, "If that is true they ought to hang him!" Then he told Herndon that he has just written to tell General Winfield Scott, the Army's General-in-Chief, "that I wished him to be prepared, immediately after my inauguration, to make arrangements at once to hold the forts, or, if they had been taken, to take them back again.

In January, while six additional states passed ordinances of secession, Lincoln left his office in the State House, preferring to hole up in a room above his law office across the street to write his inaugural address. With him, he took a copy of the Constitution, Henry Clay's speech concerning the Compromise of 1850, and Andrew Jackson's proclamation against Nullification. The nullification theory, which avows that a State has the right to ignore any federal law which does not suit the State's purposes, had been around since 1828 when Jackson feuded with South Carolina over it, and was currently back in vogue. A basic tenet of the State's Right's premise, nullification was clearly on Lincoln's mind. He asked no counsel and took none if offered to produce his remarkable statement to be delivered on the Capitol steps in March.

Perhaps the chore was complete when he quietly left Springfield in early February to visit his step-mother, Sally, at her home in Coles County. While there, he caught up with the surviving Hanks and Johnsons and visited his father's grave. Finding it unmarked and neglected, he left instructions that a stone be erected. Strange behavior, considering that not much love was lost between Thomas and his son and that Abe let his biological Mother's grave stay unmarked.

One can imagine that Abe and Sally did have another tearful farewell. Herndon reports that Sally "gave him a mother's benediction, expressing the fear that his life might be taken by his enemies." Lincoln himself had the same fear, but now as later, did not allow it to interfere with his duty.

Before Lincoln arrived home, the seceded states had met in Montgomery, Alabama to form the Confederate States of America and elected Mississippi statesman Jefferson Davis as President. At exactly the same time, a "Peace Conference" with delegates from fourteen free states and seven slave states held its first meeting in Washington hoping to resolve the sectional conflict without bloodshed.

Back in Springfield, he made his final preparations for being gone for a period. He had sold his furniture and household goods and rented his Eighth Street house, called a halt to job-seeking interviews, accepted invitations from sites in New York, New Jersey, Pennsylvanian and Ohio to make stops en route to Washington. On the afternoon of February 10, Lincoln met with Herndon to go over their partnership business. That finished, he lay down upon a couch in the office and stared at the ceiling for a few minutes. "Billy," he said at length, "how long have we been partners?" Assured that the time was over sixteen years, he arose, gathered some papers, then told Billy to let the "Lincoln and Herndon" sign at the foot of the stairs "hang there undisturbed." He told Billy, "If I live, I'm coming back sometime and we'll go right on practicing law as if nothing had ever happened." Evidently, not surviving the Presidency was much on his mind as he made ready to embark. Two things are strange about that exchange: despite these well documented premonitions of death, President (and lawyer) Lincoln died with no will, and; when Bob Lincoln came to collect his father's possessions following the assassination, Herndon refused to release the furniture. Asked about Lincoln's stated intent to continue the partnership, Herndon told Bob that neither he nor Lincoln believed it.

At 7:30 the next morning, February 11, the day before his 52nd birthday, Abe Lincoln – without wife and younger sons – accompanied only by son Bob, his secretaries, John Nicolay and John Hay and several friends started for the train depot. A New York reporter had it that he and Mary had argued that morning over a political appointment she desired her husband to make and that she lay pounding the floor in a screeching tantrum when he left. Katherine Helm says that "the early hour being inconvenient, Mrs. Lincoln decided to take a later train." Whatever the cause, she and Willie and Tad did not accompany Lincoln to the depot that morning.

"If I live, I'm coming back sometime and we'll go right on practicing law as if nothing had ever happened."
—Lincoln

Much to Abe's surprise and delight, despite the stormy day and chilling drizzle, some 1,000 people showed up to see him off. An "A. Lincoln Special" train was waiting at the Great Western Railroad depot. The depot is still there today, looking much as it did then, up to and including the chalkboard announcement that Lincoln train was "on time." After Lincoln entered the car, the crowd pressed

around the rear platform. In a moment, he reappeared and stood silently for a moment. As he had told Herndon the day before that he saw no need to prepare a farewell address, evidently he composed it on the spot. Working to control his emotions, he removed his hat and spoke slowly with an eloquence that even Abraham Lincoln rarely reached:

"My friends,

No one, not in my situation, can appreciate my feelings of sadness at this parting. To this place and the kindness of these people, I owe everything. Here I have lived a quarter of a century and have passed from a young man to an old man. Here my children have been born and one is buried. I now leave, not knowing when, or whether ever, I may return, with a task before me greater than that which rested upon Washington. Without the assistance of the Devine Being, who ever attended him, I cannot succeed. With that assistance, I cannot fail. Trusting in Him, who can go with me, and remain with you and be everywhere for good, let us confidently hope that all will yet be well. To His care commending you as I hope in your prayers you will commend me, I bid you an affectionate farewell."

Above: *From Springfield's Great Western Railroad terminal, Lincoln departed for Washington on February 11, 1860. As you can see on the chalkboard, the "Special" was on time.*

Right: *In a cold drizzle, Mr. Lincoln addressed his friends just before he left. Evidently, his eloquent remarks were off the cuff.*

As the script would dictate, just as he finished speaking, with a hiss of steam, the train lurched into motion. Lincoln was still standing at the rear platform when he disappeared around the bend, destined for strife, Civil War, heartbreak and death.

GREAT WESTERN
RAILROAD
SPRINGFIELD · ILLINOIS

THE LINCOLN DEPOT

FROM THIS BUILDING ON FEBRUARY 11, 1861 ABRAHAM LINCOLN DEPARTED SPRINGFIELD, ILLINOIS TO ASSUME THE PRESIDENCY OF THE UNITED STATES. AFTER BIDDING FAREWELL TO A NUMBER OF FRIENDS, HE DELIVERED A BRIEF, SPONTANEOUS AND MOVING FAREWELL ADDRESS TO THE CROWD, ESTIMATED AT 1,000, FROM THE REAR PLATFORM OF THE TRAIN.

ERECTED BY THE LINCOLN DEPOT, INC. AND THE ILLINOIS STATE HISTORICAL SOCIETY 1966

Relief Sculpture Panel depicting his Washington years on the Visitor Center at the Lincoln Boyhood National Memorial near Gentryville, Indiana.

WASHINGTON
1861 -1865

In your hands, my dissatisfied fellow-countrymen, and not in mine, is the momentous issue of civil war. The Government will not assail you. You can have no conflict without being yourselves the aggressors. You have no oath registered in heaven to destroy the Government, while I shall have the most solemn one to "preserve, protect, and defend it."

– President Abraham Lincoln,

March 4, 1861

DISTRICT OF COLUMBIA

The Seat of the United States Government

Where It is: On the Potomac River, tucked between Virginia, Maryland and Pennsylvania, 100 miles north of Richmond, VA and 40 miles southwest of **Baltimore, MD.**

How Lincoln Got There: A "Presidential Special" train following a zig-zag route from Springfield through Chicago, Indianapolis, Columbus and Cleveland, Buffalo, Albany and New York City, Philadelphia and Harrisburg, **and Baltimore.**

How You get There: Interstate Highways 66, 70 and 95; all roads lead to The District of Columbia.

The Trip

With the country in great crisis – seven states had already passed ordinances of secession – Mr. Lincoln felt that he must let the people have a look at him. So, what would have ordinarily been a train trip of two days was transformed into a two week ordeal by the invitations the President-elect had accepted to appear at various points in Illinois, Ohio, New York, New Jersey and Pennsylvania.

In addition to addressing the civic groups and state legislatures for which he had bargained, crowds pressed around the Presidential car at every stop. Mary, Willie and Tad joined the Presidential party the day after it left Springfield at Indianapolis. They celebrated Lincoln's birthday as privately as possible, Mary giving her traditional comments which ended, "I feel so grateful to your Mother." In addition to the family and his secretaries, political crony Norman P. Judd, old friend, and on this occasion bodyguard, Ward Hill Lamon, and Lincoln's "military friend," Elmer Ellsworth were aboard.

The trip went smoothly until the party reached Philadelphia on February 21. At that place, detective Allan Pinkerton (who would become the Union Army's chief espionage officer and hence the father of the Secret Service) came aboard to warn of a plot to assassinate Lincoln in Baltimore. Pinkerton did not get direct access to the President-elect, of course, but had to tell his story to Judd and Lamon first. Those two gentlemen took Pinkerton to Lincoln where he repeated the story and urged Lincoln to leave right away so as to arrive in Baltimore unexpectedly.

Lincoln flatly refused to consider that idea as he was scheduled to raise a flag over Independence Hall the next morning and be at Harrisburg to address the Pennsylvania Legislature in the afternoon. He displayed no distress over the news and informed all present that he fully well intended to keep his appointments.

This story might have ended there except that William Seward, incoming Secretary of State had independently discovered the same plot and dispatched his son, Fredrick, to inform Lincoln. Reluctantly, then, Lincoln acceded to their plan to slip surreptitiously through Baltimore ahead of schedule, "unless there are other reasons besides fear of ridicule" for not doing so. He would, indeed, receive the anticipated ridicule, later being accused of cowardice and passing to Washington City in disguise.

On the 22nd, having fulfilled his appearance obligations, Lincoln slipped out of Harrisburg at 6 PM accompanied only by Lamon. Only a few of the official party, including Mrs. Lincoln, knew of the plan. All the telegraph wires were cut so that there would be no warning to whoever might be waiting in Baltimore. The usually jovial Lincoln was quiet during the all night ride, "indulging in only a joke or two, in an undertone." Pinkerton's agents, posted

The Washington Monument at night.

along line the signaled the "all clear" until the train pulled into Baltimore at 3:30 AM. Here, Pinkerton joined Lincoln and Lamon in the car as it was transferred to the Baltimore and Ohio tracks. At 6 AM, the train arrived in Washington City where Lincoln, Pinkerton and Lamon were amazed to find Illinois Congressman Elihu Washburne awaiting their arrival. Seward, aware of the plot, and in a panic after discovering that the telegraph wires had been cut, had enlisted Washburne to help him meet every train. The newly arrived trio accompanied Washburne in his waiting carriage to the Willard Hotel where Lincoln had made arrangements to live until he moved to the White House.

The city Lincoln saw that February morning was little different from what he had seen back in '47 when he was an Illinois Congressman. The streets were still largely unpaved, open sewer pipes from the houses emptied into the streets, the old wooden Capitol Dome, now much out of proportion, still graced the expanded building and the top

To this day, one can see the difference in the color of the stone about a third of the way up marking the halt in construction due to the Civil War.

of the Washington Monument was only 150 feet above the ground. Construction on the monument, begun in 1848, was at a halt due to lack of funds and remained suspended during the war. After the war, the same funding problem kept it uncompleted until 1884. To this very day, one

Abraham Lincoln

can still see a difference in the color of the stone about one-third of the way up to its 555 foot peak.

Only a few minutes after the Presidential party was conducted to Parlor Number 6, Seward puffed in, out of breath, distressed that he had missed the train's arrival. Lincoln and Seward breakfasted together before beginning the day's official duties, the first of which, maybe not officially, was to telegraph Mary Lincoln that he had arrived safely.

The actual first official duty of the President-elect is to call on the President. A cabinet meeting was in progress when Lincoln arrived at the White House. President Buchanan rushed down to meet Lincoln and escorted him upstairs to meet the Cabinet members, several of whom, most notably Attorney General Edwin Stanton, exhibited an obvious contempt for the folksy Westerner. Lincoln had not forgotten how Stanton had insulted him in Cincinnati, but was willing to evaluate the man's abilities in a new light.

Next on the list of duties was to pay a call on General Winfield Scott. "Old Fuss and Feathers" was considered the greatest military man of his time and although he was well past his prime at age 75, Lincoln and the country would depend on his judgment in the developing crisis. General Scott was not at home, so Lincoln and Seward returned to Williard's just in time to greet Mary Lincoln and the boys.

Notified that the Peace Conference delegates would like to see him, Lincoln scheduled that meeting for 9 PM. In the afternoon, after a meeting with an Illinois delegation headed by Senator Stephen Douglas, came venerable political manipulator Francis P. Blair and his son, Montgomery who was an (successful, as it turned out) applicant for Postmaster General. After dinner with Hannibal Hamlin at Seward's home, Lincoln returned

The Washington Monument was unfinished when Lincoln arrived to take office. Library of Congress

[abolitionist William Lloyd] Garrisons." Perhaps, as he was not personally involved with the fate of either of those men, Lincoln took the Virginian's comments as an indictment of the Republican Party, but when he laconically replied, "I believe John Brown was hanged and Mr. Garrison imprisoned," the room fell momentarily silent. After some further discussion, Seddon attacked again.

Finally, frustrated by Lincoln's cool logic, Seddon (who would become Confederate Secretary of War) thundered, "Then you will yield to the just demands of the South. You will leave her to control her own institutions. You will admit slave states into the Union on the same conditions as free states. You will not go to war on account of slavery."

Just as coolly as before, Lincoln said, "I shall take an oath. I shall swear that as President of the United States – of all the United States – that I will ... preserve, protect and defend the Constitution of the United States....It is not the Constitution as I would like to have it, but as it is, that is to be defended."

One could have heard the proverbial pin drop as the delegates digested that bit of Lincoln wisdom. These gentlemen had apparently been promised an evening's

to Willard's where a huge crowd accosted him in the hallway.

The Peace delegates, headed by ex-President John Tyler and soon-to-be Treasury Secretary Salmon P. Chase, arrived as scheduled. Chase, the former Ohio Senator and Governor had been Lincoln's rival for the Presidential nomination and was obviously still smarting over being passed over as he introduced Lincoln to each delegate. A witness observed that it was Chase who looked more Presidential, an assessment with which Chase would have readily agreed. That idea would have dismayed Seward who thought it was he that should be president. As successful politicians do, Lincoln knew something about each man to whom he was introduced and casually displayed his political knowledge and skill. Mr. Rives, retired Virginia politician, remarked that he could do little while Lincoln could do much. "Everything depends on you," Rives opined.

Lincoln disagreed. "My course is as plain as a turnpike road. It is marked out by the Constitution."

Evidently somewhat miffed, Virginian James Seddon attacked the President-elect. "It is not of your professions we complain....it is your sins of omission – your failure to enforce the laws – to suppress your John Browns and your

Lincoln's party stayed at Willard's Hotel in Washington for two weeks prior to his inauguration. Library of Congress

The restored Willard's is still one of the most elegant hotels in our nation's Capital.

entertainment at the discomfiture of the country bumpkin in the presence of such refined gentlemen as themselves. As it was, they went away much impressed with the logic and determination of the man who would be President.

Inauguration Day was scheduled for March 4. With his address polished and ready and the Cabinet selections made, it would seem that Mr. Lincoln had little to do except greet the hordes who called on him. But, the rarified atmosphere of Presidential politics allows scant respites. In addition to the job-seekers, the President-elect was besieged by intriguers seeking to induce him to include or exclude some person from his cabinet. At the top of that list were Seward's friends seeking to exclude Chase and Chase's friends asking the opposite. Lincoln had decided, of courses, to name both of these men – political rivals not only of himself, but each other – because he felt the country would need the strongest men available. Mr. Lincoln of Illinois, as his friends knew, was strong enough to mold the rivals into a smoothly-oiled machine.

Finally, on March 2, he grew so weary that he banned uninvited callers. Just when everything should have been calming down, a letter arrived from Seward asking that his name be withdrawn from consideration for the Cabinet. Perhaps that gentleman had discovered that Lincoln was a stronger personality and more forceful politician that he had suspected and hence he would not become the de-facto President as he'd planned. Lincoln wanted Seward in his cabinet, and did not intend to let his rival win this first test. Before he could respond to Seward's request, a previously scheduled dinner for William H. Seward, Salmon P. Chase, Gideon Welles, Montgomery Blair, Simon Cameron, Caleb B. Smith, and Edward Bates – whose names he would forward to Senate as prospective cabinet members – was held March 3.

Inauguration

The big day dawned cloudy and cold. Early in the morning, Lincoln sent a note to Seward asking him to rescind his withdrawal, which he did a day later. Later, he met with various politicians and friends and possibly added a few finishing touches to his address. Shortly before noon, President Buchanan arrived at Willard's Hotel. In a few minutes, the out-going and the incoming

Abraham Lincoln

Presidents left the hotel for a short carriage ride to the Capitol where the Senate was waiting. Due to rumors of assassination attempts, the streets were lined with soldiers, armed riflemen manned rooftops and more soldiers near the Capitol stood by their cannon, lanyards in hand. The Presidential party entered the Senate chamber where the two Presidents took front row seats as out-going Vice President Breckenridge administered the oath of office to Hannibal Hamlin. By 1 PM, the weather had cleared, so Lincoln walked onto the East Portico steps in bright sunshine. A crowd of spectators surrounded the inaugural platform constructed beneath the unfinished Capitol Dome. He was dressed in an all new custom-made suit, topped by a high silk hat and set off by a cane with a golden head. Another part of the Lincoln myth is that he stashed the cane under the table but, as he could find nowhere to place his hat, Stephen Douglas (who was, in fact, on the platform) stepped forward, took the hat and held it during the address. That's a great story – evidently Mary Lincoln told it to her sister Emilie, so that Emilie's

daughter, Katherine, repeated it in her biography of Mary; it is unclear whether the event actually happened.

Once again, Abraham Lincoln displayed his ability to say much in a few words. He said, in part:

"Apprehension seems to exist among the people of the Southern States, that by the accession of a Republican Administration, their property, and their peace, and personal security, are to be endangered. There has never been any reasonable cause for such apprehension. . . .

"I take the official oath today, with no mental reservations, and with no purpose to construe the Constitution or laws, by any hypercritical rules. . . . I hold, that in contemplation of universal law, and of the Constitution, the Union of these States is perpetual. . . .

"It follows from these views that no State, upon its own mere motion, can lawfully get out of the Union. . . I therefore consider that in view of the Constitution and the laws, the Union is unbroken; and, to the extent of my ability, I shall take care, . . . that the laws of the Union be faithfully executed in all the States. . . .

"In doing this there needs to be no bloodshed or violence; and there shall be none unless it be forced upon the national authority. . . . One section of our country believes slavery is right, and ought to be extended, while the other believes it is wrong, and ought not to be extended. This is the only substantial dispute. . . .

The Chief Magistrate derives all his authority from the people, and they have conferred none upon him to fix terms for the separation of the States. . . .

"If it were admitted that you who are dissatisfied, hold the right side in the dispute, there still is no single good reason for precipitate action. . . . In your hands, my dissatisfied fellow countrymen, and not in mine, is the momentous issue of civil war. . . .

"I am loath to close. We are not enemies, but friends. We must not be enemies. Though passion may have strained, it must not break our bonds of affection. The mystic chords of memory, stretching from every battlefield and patriot grave to every living heart and hearthstone all over this broad land, will yet swell the chorus of the Union when again touched, as surely they will be, by the better angels of our nature."

The address, which lasted barely half an hour, met with scattered and unenthusiastic applause. Evidently Lincoln's policies and sage advice were not what either section of the country wanted to hear. Chief Justice Roger B. Taney then stepped forward to administer the oath of office. While the Marine band played "God Save Our President," the participants began the procession to the White House.

Henry Watterson, who, after a stint in the Confederate Army would become one of the most influential journalists of his age, was one of the few who was impressed with the

Opposite page: *The unfinished new Capitol Dome dominates the skyline as Lincoln delivers his first inaugural address on March 4, 1861. Library of Congress* **Above:** *The Capitol Dome still dominates Washington's sky.*

The oldest known photograph of the White House shows how it looked in 1860, a few months before the Lincolns moved in. The statue of Thomas Jefferson in the center of the drive is now in the Capitol Rotunda. Library of Congress

new President. "He delivered that inaugral address as if he had been delivering inaugural addresses all his life," said Watterson.

Unfortunately the nation paid little heed to what Mr. Lincoln said that day.

Crisis

As the Lincoln party swapped the gaiety of Willard's Hotel for the gravity awaiting in the White House, "Old Fuss and Feathers," General Winfield Scott was a worried man. Although the rumored explosive demolition of the speakers' platform had not occurred, still there was a lot of territory to protect. With less than seven hundred soldiers at his immediate command, the streets thronged with men of uncertain loyalties and a rebel army gathering across the Potomac, General Scott had ample cause for concern.

So did the President. After his first dinner in the White House, which was interrupted by a delegation of New York merry-makers, he and Mrs. Lincoln arrived at the Inaugural Ball about 11 PM. After the Grand March, he did not dance, even in "the worst way," but left his wife dancing with Stephen Douglas to return to the White House. As soon as he entered, about 1 AM, he was handed a note from Major Robert Anderson – Lincoln's Black Hawk War commander – in command of besieged Fort Sumter in Charleston Bay. Anderson informed the President that the fort's provisions would not last until any relief could reach South Carolina, so he would soon be forced to surrender.

Busy with patronage and other administrative matters, the President was unable to consult with General Scott until March 9. At that time, General Scott agreed that "evacuation seems almost inevitable."

On Sunday, March 10, the Lincolns made their first visit to the New York Avenue Presbyterian Church which

Abraham Lincoln

dominates the landscape at New York Avenue and H Street. Mary Lincoln had requested a plat of the church before coming to Washington and chosen a pew location. That pew, where the family sat throughout the remainder of the President's life, is still very much in evidence today. Lincoln did not attend church with the regularity his wife did, but he did develop a relationship with the minister, Dr. Phineas Gurley.

The situation at Fort Sumter was critical. Although the precedent was set – State troops had seized Federal property, not only forts, but arsenals and mints – in Alabama, Georgia, Florida and Louisiana in the waning days of the Buchanan administration without resistance. Fort Sumter, with the nation's eyes focused on it, was a different case and Lincoln was no Buchanan. In his inaugural address, President Lincoln had promised "your government will not assail you," he had also said that the Government would

protect its property. Nevertheless, he did not intend to let Federal property, including Sumter, go. As soon as the Cabinet was in place, he sent a note, through the Secretary of War, to General Scott. "I am directed by the President to say that he desires you to exercise all possible vigilance for the maintenance of all the places within the military department of the United States, and to promptly call upon all the departments of Government for the means necessary to that end."

The difficulty lay in maintaining Federal property while not precipitating a shooting war and at the same time appeasing the non-seceded states – a delicate chore, indeed and Major Anderson's supply situation had set a time limit for some kind of solution. Lincoln could alleviate the crisis by ordering the fort evacuated, of course, but feared that would be viewed as displaying weakness of resolve. In the end, the President decided to try to re-supply the fort.

On April 4, Lincoln met with Virginia Unionists to discuss the proposition that if the Federal Government would give up Fort Sumter, Virginia, which had passed an ordinance of secession, would not ratify it and hence not secede from the Union. Nothing came of this meeting, but how delicious to consider the different course history would had have taken had Virginia remained in the Union!

On a more domestic scale, about that same time Abraham Lincoln received his first paycheck as President. The salary was $25,000 per year, so his monthly draw was a little over $2,000. As he had not brought sufficient funds along initially, he had been forced to make arrangements for deferred payment of his $773.75 hotel bill, so Willard's received a chunk of that first check. Over the course of his terms as President, Mr. Lincoln invested a large portion of his salary in war bonds.

While the President pondered his dilemma, General Beauregard, having recently resigned as Commandant at West Point to accept command of the Confederate forces surrounding Fort Sumter, demanded, in a gentlemanly way, Anderson's surrender. Anderson refused, but told Beauregard's aides, "Gentlemen, if you do not batter the fort to pieces about us, we shall be starved out in a few days."

With that information, Beauregard offered again, on

The Lincoln family sat in this second row pew in Washington's New York Avenue Presbyterian Church.

April 12, generous surrender terms. This time, Anderson replied that he would evacuate the fort on the 15th, unless he "received supplies or contradictory instruction" in the meantime. Beauregard, a hot-blooded Creole, would wait no longer even had he not had orders to attack. When he sent his aides in, he had directed them to tell Anderson that if he refused again, bombardment would begin at 4:20 AM, April 12.

"…This issue embraces more than the fate of these United States. It presents to the whole family of man the question of whether a constitutional republic or democracy – a government of the people by the same people – can or cannot maintain its territorial integrity against its own domestic foes."
—Lincoln

Beauregard was as good as his word. As soon as the aides were safely out of range, a mortar battery fired on Sumter at 4:30 AM. The Union batteries within the fort promptly answered in kind. The shooting war was on.

The result was a brilliant piece of statesmanship on Lincoln's part. He had kept his promise, "the government will not assail you," yet maintained the national integrity and refused to be bullied.

In Washington, the President was kept abreast of developments via telegraph. While he tried to maintain a "business as usual" attitude by greeting visitors, signing papers and attending to routine matters, his stomach was, no doubt, churning. Only months later did he reveal his feelings, telling Congress, "…This issue embraces more than the fate of these United States. It presents to the whole family of man the question of whether a constitutional republic or democracy – a government of the people by the same people – can or cannot maintain its territorial integrity against its own domestic foes." The man saw the issue clearly!

The Rebel artillery blasted Fort Sumter to rubble leaving its garrison no choice other than surrender. After about forty hours of bombardment, Major Anderson and his men, blackened and exhausted, evacuated the fort. In the ensuing meeting with the attackers, it was determined that the fight had been bloodless – not a man of either party

had been killed and a total of nine were wounded, none seriously. Beauregard allowed – it was a gentlemanly war at this point – the Federal garrison to raise the Stars and Stripes for a final salute. One of the Union gun crew was killed by an accidental explosion during the salute.

Abraham Lincoln

A day later President Lincoln called for 75,000 volunteers to serve an optimistic 90 day tour of duty. The patriotic men of the Northern states responded quickly, but until they could organize, Washington lay undefended as only a handful of regular Army troops were deployed in the areas. So obvious was the opportunity that Lincoln told General Scott that if he were General Beauregard, "I'd take Washington." The War Department offered arms to anyone willing to help defend Washington City. Seeing the same opportunity, Kentucky's redoubtable Mexican War hero, Cassius M. Clay, in town to collect some office as a reward for his campaign efforts, decided to take action. Clay organized 'The Clay Battalion' for the defense of the city and called on the President in the White House on April 22nd, armed with three pistols and "my accustomed Bowie knife." Evidently, Clay's presence did not cause Lincoln to feel as secure as Clay had hoped as he continued to fret about the safety of Washington. Lincoln did, however, have his picture taken with Clay and some of his "battalion" on April 29. Clay says that after his men were relieved by regular army troops "being of no longer use in Washington, I yielded up my command" and claims that the President gave him a Colt's revolver "as a testimony of his regard." Cassius Clay had previously refused a post as Minister to Spain, but now accepted Lincoln's offer to serve as Minister to Russia.

Over the years, much has been made of Lincoln's violations of the Constitution he was sworn to enforce. That he is guilty is shown by this order to General Scott:

April 27, 1861

To the Commanding General of the Army of the United States:

You are engaged in repressing an insurrection against the laws of the United States. If at any point

on or in the vicinity of the [any] military line, which is now [or which shall be] used between the City of Philadelphia and the City of Washington, via Perryville, Annapolis City, and Annapolis Junction, you find resistance which renders it necessary to suspend the writ of *Habeas Corpus* for the public safety, you, personally or through the officer in command at the point where the [at which] resistance occurs, are authorized to suspend that writ.

For the salvation of the Union, we are indeed fortunate that we had a President who recognized that such extraordinary times required such extraordinary measures.

When Lincoln was nominated for President, his "military friend" Elmer Ellsworth was studying law with Lincoln and Herndon in Springfield. Ellsworth was a New Yorker who had organized a "Zouave" unit in Chicago. Wearing the baggy red pants favored by French colonial troops, Ellsworth trained them until they became a national champion drill team before he came to Lincoln's office to study. Going along to Washington as body guard, Ellsworth became one of Lincoln's favorites. Eventually, Lincoln had Ellsworth appointed Colonel of a brigade recruited from the New York fire department. By the time Lincoln and son Tad watched them go through their paces behind the Capitol on May 7, Ellsworth had outfitted them in the "Zouave" uniforms, so they became New York's "Fire Zouaves."

When Virginia officially seceded from the Union on May 23rd, the Union's first order of business was to secure the Potomac Bridges, beginning at 2 AM on the 24th. That chore accomplished, Colonel Ellsworth and his Zouaves were moved by steamer from their camp down river to Alexandria with an eye toward capturing that city. After a bloodless landing, Ellsworth ordered some of his men to take the railroad station while he and a few other soldiers went to secure the telegraph office. While doing this, Ellsworth noticed a Confederate flag flying above the Marshall House Inn. He and three others quickly went up the stairs to cut down the flag. Flag in hand, he was on the way down the stairs when the owner, James W. Jackson, killed (many period accounts say "murdered") him with a shotgun blast to the chest.

Lincoln openly wept over his friend's death. After

he and Mary went to the Washington Navy Yard to view the body, he received some visitors in the afternoon but excused himself as unable to see anyone. Lincoln returned to the Navy Yard in the evening and arranged for an honor guard to bring his friend's body to the White House where it lay in state in the East Room until the funeral services at noon on May 25. Billed as the

Robert Todd Lincoln about 1880. Library of Congress

first man to fall for the Union cause, Ellsworth's body was then taken to the New York City Hall where thousands of Union supporters came to pay respects. Ellsworth was then buried in Hudson View Cemetery in his hometown of Mechanicville, New York. Later Lincoln wrote Ellsworth's parents, "My acquaintance with him began less than two years ago; yet through the latter half of the intervening period, it was as intimate as the disparity of our ages, and my engrossing engagements, would permit."

The Marshall House is one of many sites we cannot still see. Located at the corner of Pitt and King Streets in Alexandria, there's a Holiday Inn there now.

The dubious honor of being the first man to die in the war is claimed for many, but the death of Colonel Ellsworth was the first to bring the cruelty home personally to the President. It would not be the last.

Bob

When Lincoln was campaigning, billed as The Rail Splitter, England's Prince of Wales (later Edward VII) had recently toured America. Quick with the pun, the American press dubbed his American counterpart, Bob Lincoln, The Prince of Rails.

In one of the strangest coincidences in history, Robert

T. Lincoln's life was once saved by Edwin Booth, brother of the Presidential assassin. The incident happened at a railroad station in Jersey City on one of Bob's trips to Washington during the war. As Bob related the story, he was standing on the platform when he was pressed against the train cars by the crowd. "In this situation, the train began to move and … I was twisted off my feet…. [I] was personally helpless when … I was quickly pulled … to a secure footing on the platform. Upon turning to thank my rescuer, I saw that it was Edwin Booth…." Bob recognized Edwin, also a famous actor, and despite his grief when John Wilkes killed the President, Bob was always grateful to Edwin.

On May 31, 1861 the Prince (on vacation from Harvard,) and Presidential secretaries John Hay and John G. Nicolay, evidently had enough influence with someone to obtain passes allowing them to cross the military lines, over Long Bridge into Virginia and to the Custis mansion, (Arlington) home of Robert E. Lee. Lee, holding the rank of Colonel in the United States Army, was one of its most respected officers and had been in command of the detachment which captured John Brown during his 1859 Harper's Ferry raid.

Earlier in April, Lee had refused Lincoln's offer to command the Union Army and resigned his commission to join the Rebel forces after Virginia seceded. The mansion, which was intended as a living memorial to our first president, was built by Washington's adopted grandson, George Washington Parke Custis. Mr. Custis' daughter, Mary Anna, had married Lee on June 13, 1831 in her father's home overlooking Washington City. Upon Custis' death, Arlington became the Lees' property.

After Virginia ratified secession, Yankee troops commanded by Brigadier General Irvin McDowell, established fortifications around Arlington House, including what was Fort Whipple then and is now Fort Myer. These positions were being occupied when Bob and the secretaries made their visit.

Two years later, the federal government established

Memorial to Civil War Unknown Union Dead in Mrs. Robert E. Lee's rose garden at Arlington.

Tomb site of Robert Todd Lincoln, his wife, Mary Harlan Lincoln and their son, Abraham Lincoln II in Arlington National Cemetery.

Freedman's Village, a model community for freed slaves on the property. Some 1,100 freed slaves were granted land which they farmed and lived on until after the War.

In 1864 the federal government confiscated the property as the taxes were not paid in person by either Mr. or Mrs. Lee as the law required. The property was offered subsequently at auction on January 11, 1864 when it was purchased by the Government, lending an air of legitimacy to the whole business.

By that time, Brigadier General Montgomery C. Meigs, in command of the garrison at Arlington House, apparently thought it would be a good joke on General Lee to bury Yankee soldiers in his wife's rose garden. Accordingly, Private William Henry Christman of the 67th Pennsylvania Infantry, was the first serviceman interred at Arlington on May 13, 1864. A month later, the property would become Arlington National Cemetery.

In 1866 a memorial was erected in Mary Lee's rose garden to honor the Union dead. Beneath the tomb-like monument "repose the bones of two-thousand-two-hundred-eleven unknown soldiers gathered after the War from the fields of Bull Run….."

After the War, General Lee, being *persona non grata* with the Government, kept a low profile and attempted to be a model citizen aware of the legions who admired him. Accordingly, neither he nor his wife ever challenged the government take-over. However, following Lee's death in 1870, his eldest son, George Washington Custis Lee, brought an action in Circuit Court to evict the Government from his property. Custis Lee claimed

that the land had been illegally confiscated and that, according to his grandfather's will, he was the legal owner. In December 1882, the U.S. Supreme Court, in a 5-4 decision, returned the property to Custis Lee, holding that it had been confiscated without due process, much, no doubt, to the chagrin of the Government.

Rather than attempt to move the graves, Congress purchased the property from Lee for $150,000 in 1883. At that time, it became a military reservation and Freedman's Village was removed.

Today, Arlington National Cemetery occupies 612 acres of Virginia overlooking Washington and is the final resting place of servicemen and women representing every war in which the United States has been involved. Among the nearly 500,000 people buried there are Robert Todd Lincoln, his wife Mary Harlan Lincoln and their son, Abraham Lincoln II. Bob Lincoln qualified for burial in a National Cemetery by virtue of serving on General U.S. Grant's staff for a short period near the end of the Civil War and as Secretary of War from 1881 to 1885 under Presidents Garfield and Arthur.

When Abraham Lincoln II – "Jack" he was to the family – died in 1890, Bob Lincoln initially buried him in the Lincoln tomb in Springfield. Bob gave all appearances of intending to rest there himself, but upon Bob's death in 1926, his wife decided that, although there was a space for him in the Lincoln tomb in Springfield, IL, he had earned his own spot in history, so she opted that he be buried at Arlington rather than where his father, mother and siblings rest. Subsequently, in 1930, she had Jack's body moved to Arlington, as well. When Bob hiked up to General Lee's house on that lovely day in May 1861, he surely never dreamed he'd walked across his final resting place in what is now Section 31 of Arlington National Cemetery.

> *"I, Abraham Lincoln, President of the United States, of my own knowledge, know that it is untrue that any member of my family holds treasonable communications with the enemy."*
>
> –Lincoln

Little Sister

Mary Lincoln's "Little Sister," Emilie married Bardstown, Kentucky native Benjamin Hardin Helm in 1856. Helm was an 1851 graduate of West Point who had served briefly in the Army before his health forced him to retire to Kentucky where he obtained a law degree. On some legal business, Ben spent a week with the Lincolns in Springfield in 1857. Although he and his brother-in-law differed politically, they became good friends. After a term in the Legislature, Helm was appointed assistant inspector general of the Kentucky State Guard in 1860.

On April 27, 1861, Ben Helm appeared at the White House in response to President Lincoln's invitation. The President handed Helm an envelope and asked that he consider the offer. The envelope contained a commission as Paymaster of the Union Army in the rank of Major – a plum assignment. After much soul searching, Helm politely refused the offer, preferring (as Mrs. Lincoln's brother, three half-brothers and three brothers-in-law did) to cast his lot with the other side. By September, Helm was Colonel of the 1st regiment of the Confederate Kentucky Cavalry. After participating in the battle at Shiloh in April 1862, he was promoted to Brigadier General serving in that rank until he was killed at Chickamauga on September 20, 1863.

Of all the Todd offspring, Emilie was the prettiest and Mary's favorite companion. Lincoln himself, quite fond of Emilie and her husband, was grief stricken upon hearing of Ben's death. As Emilie was stranded behind Confederate lines, Lincoln intervened, ordering her and her daughter, Katherine, to the White House. Tad, entertaining Katherine, picked up a picture of his father. "This is the President," he announced.

"No," countered Katherine, referring to the Confederate President, "Mr. Davis is the President."

Despite her love for the Lincolns, Emilie remained an unreconstructed rebel for all of her long life and hence was uncomfortable in the White House. "Sister and I cannot open our hearts to each other as freely as we would like," she lamented. Lincoln, accused of harboring "that little rebel," defended her presence, but she eventually asked the President for a pass to allow her to return to Kentucky. When she clashed with Kentucky's Military Governor, Stephen Burbridge (being far from the only Kentuckian to

Emilie Todd Helm. Courtesy of Hardin County History Museum.

do so), she appealed to the President for help. After Lincoln told Burbridge to deal with her the same as any other, she fired off an angry letter: "I have been a quiet citizen and request only the right which humanity and justice always gives to widows and orphans. I also would remind you that your minié bullets have made us what we are." After that, Emilie was estranged from Abe and Mary Lincoln, never speaking to either again. Apparently passions cooled or perhaps she desired to show affection for Bob Lincoln after he had helped her become postmistress of Elizabethtown, but she did, as previously noted, agree to be present at the Lincoln ceremonies at Hodgenville in 1909.

Emilie Helm attended many of the Confederate Veteran reunions and was given the title "Mother of the Brigade" by the former soldiers of the First Kentucky – the famed "Orphan" Brigade of which her husband had been commander.

She never remarried and wore mourning clothes for her husband for the remainder of her life. She was 93 years old when she died and was buried in the Todd plot at the Lexington City Cemetery.

In December 1861, as Congress knew more about how to run a war than the military (just as they do today,) a Joint Committee on the Conduct of the War was established. The politics of that group is fascinating and a source of great irritation to President Lincoln and his administration, but is mentioned here only because Lincoln got wind of a secret meeting being held to discuss rumors that the White House was harboring Rebel spies. Just as the meeting was called to order, the President appeared, hat in hand. Needless to say, the room fell silent. Finally, Lincoln, speaking slowly, said, "I, Abraham Lincoln, President of the United States, of my own knowledge, know that it is untrue that any member of my family holds treasonable communications with the enemy." That put an end to the official investigation of the Todds in the White House.

Major General George B. McClellan

When the actual shooting war began in April 1861, Winfield Scott, veteran of every conflict since the War of 1812 – and hero of most of them – was the General-in-Chief of the Army. Past 75 years of age, gout-ridden to the extent that Lincoln met him downstairs in the White House to save him climbing the stairs, and so corpulent he could not sit a horse, Scott was clearly not physically fit for active command, so a replacement was sought. Before we leave General Scott, though, it is worth noting that he is the man who conceived the strategy known as the Anaconda Plan to squeeze the life out of the Confederacy. Although that plan met with great ridicule when he announced it,

President Lincoln faces Major General George McClellan in 1863. Library of Congress

Abraham Lincoln. Library of Congress

charged with the defense of Washington. When General Scott retired on November 1, Lincoln promoted McClellan to General-in-Chief.

Little Mac was an excellent organizer and trainer. Within weeks, he had the demoralized army whipped into fighting trim, well-organized, well-equipped and in high morale. The soldiers loved him and he, in return, loved his army. As it turned out, he loved it too much to risk it in battle. Additionally, he refused to share his plans with the President – "He'd tell Tad and then the whole country would know," said McClellan.

On the evening of November 13, 1861, President Lincoln, Secretary Seward and John Hay went to General McClellan's residence on some business. Informed that the General was not at home, but would soon return, they decided to wait. After about an hour, McClellan entered the front door and was informed that the President was waiting in the parlor. On his way upstairs, he did not even glance in as he passed the doorway where the three gentlemen waited. After another 30 minutes, Seward asked the valet to again tell the General that they were waiting. The valet said that McClellan had gone to bed!

John Hay reports that he spoke with the President about the incident on the way to the White House and that Lincoln simply said that it was better at this time not to be making points of etiquette. Lincoln later told someone that he "would hold the General's horse if it would bring victories." A man of great patience was Abraham Lincoln.

But not infinite patience. As McClellan would not risk his army in battle and would not divulge his plans (he said he had one) to the President – his Commander-in-Chief, his constant complaining of being outnumbered wore thin with Lincoln. When a newspaper man asked Lincoln to estimate the size of the Confederate Army, without hesitation, he put it at an incredible 1,200,000 men. Asked how he arrived at such an outlandish figure, Lincoln replied that he knew the Army of the Potomac had 300,000 men and General McClellan assured him that he was outnumbered four to one.

So slow to action was Little Mac that Lincoln, who,

General Scott did live long enough to see his blockade plan effectively used to defeat the rebellion.

After Robert E. Lee refused the command, political wrangling brought the honor to Irwin McDowell. Events and political pressure forced McDowell to attack at Bull Run (known to the Confederates as Manassas Junction) on July 21 before the Army was ready, resulting in humiliating defeat and McDowell's removal from command.

The man who had distinguished himself already in the conflict was Major General George B. McClellan. A short man, "Little Mac" was a West Pointer who had served in the Mexican War before he resigned to become chief engineer of the Illinois Central Railroad, where he may have had dealings with Lincoln the lawyer. At the outbreak of war, McClellan came back to the Army, assuming the rank of Major General. As the country was hungry for a hero and McClellan had enjoyed some early success in what would soon become West Virginia, President Lincoln placed McClellan in charge of the Army of the Potomac

as President, studied military tactics and had a plan of his own, telegraphed McClellan that if he did not plan to be using his Army, he (Lincoln) would like to borrow it.

General McClellan's ill-conceived and therefore disastrous Peninsula Campaign in 1862 and his poor performance at Antietam in the fall of that year, led to his removal (temporarily) from command after he had been given more chances than anyone other than Abe Lincoln would have allowed.

Willie

Billy Herndon said that Abe Lincoln was the most permissive parent he ever knew. Perhaps having lost one son to death already persuaded the parents to let the boys enjoy themselves, unrestrained by parental interference, and Billy had horror tales of the havoc the Lincoln boys wreaked on the law office. Mr. Lincoln's attitude did not change when he became President. Bob was away at school, but Willie and Tad ran roughshod over the place, interrupting Cabinet meetings, bossing the staff around and creating general mayhem, without correction from, and sometimes encouraged by, their father. Both Mary and Abe were fond of all the boys, but each had his own personality; Willie was more like his mother while Tad was a fun-loving imp like his father on the circuit and Bob was a Todd, through and through.

The tutor, employed in the White House, found Willie a willing and apt pupil, but Tad considered the lessons just something to be endured. Indeed, Tad did not

THE LINCOLN FAMILY IN 1861.

Despite the fact that a family portrait would have done much to dispel the despotic image Lincoln's political opponents tried to create, no such photograph has ever been found. This lithograph is a composite made from easily recognizable photographs of the individuals. Library of Congress

learn to read until after his father's death. "Let him run, there's plenty of time for him to learn his letters," was Lincoln's attitude.

A few days before Christmas, Willie, fond of playing outdoors even in bad weather, fell ill, apparently with a cold. As January crawled by, giving way to February's dreary days, his condition worsened; he suffered with a fever and grew weaker daily. Finally, Doctor Stone concluded that the child was better and, while still ill, was in no immediate danger and would soon be running about the place again. Accordingly, no change was made in the White House social schedule.

On the evening of a reception, Willie took a turn for the worse. In a long silk dress, Mary sat at his bedside, holding his hand, while her husband stood nearby. Reluctantly, she released the child's hand to go downstairs on Mr. Lincoln's arm. During the reception, she left the festivities several times to dash upstairs checking on his condition. All the parents' concern and the doctor's care were to no avail; on February 20, 1862, two months past his 11th birthday, William Wallace Lincoln died. Mrs. Lincoln was washed away with grief. Mr. Lincoln came into the room, lifted the covers from his dead child's face and sobbed. To no one in particular, he said. "My poor boy, he was too good for this world. God has called him home. I know that he is much better off in Heaven, but then we loved him so. It is hard, hard to have him die."

Willie was buried in Oak Hill Cemetery in Georgetown. Lincoln's job as President and Commander in Chief did not stop, or even pause, but from Willie's death on, the sadness which always attended him was deeper. Some observers thought that Willie's death caused Lincoln's religious convictions to grow deeper as well.

When President Lincoln was assassinated, Willie's casket was disinterred so that it could travel on the train back to Springfield with his father's body.

"Gentlemen, I have, as you are aware, thought a great deal about the relation of this war to slavery.... I made a promise to my self, and to my Maker. The Rebel army is now driven out and I am going to fulfill that promise."

—Lincoln

Emancipation

In the summer of 1862, although the war occupied most of his time, slavery was on the President's mind. As recently as his inaugural address he had repeated the declaration that he had no intent of interfering with slavery where it existed and that he felt he had no Constitutional authority to do so. In August, his famous letter told New York *Tribune* editor, Horace Greeley "My paramount object in this struggle is to save the Union, and it is not either to save or destroy slavery. If I could save the Union without freeing any salve, I would do it; if I could save it by freeing all the slaves, I would do it; if I could save it by freeing some and leaving others alone, I would also do that." Sometime that summer, he evidently changed his mind, although his friend Speed says Lincoln's mind was set long before any announcement.

In mid-July riding with two Cabinet members in a carriage, the President mentioned freeing the slaves, stating that he felt it had become "a military necessity absolutely essential for the salvation of the Union." That comment is exactly in line with what he had written to Mr. Greeley concerning saving the Union. The Secretaries were taken aback, all previous mention of the topic had met with "prompt and emphatic denouncement," but with the war going badly for the Union, Mr. Lincoln wished to deprive the South of the military and economic benefits of slave labor. Additionally, as the probability of England and France lending aid to the Confederacy appeared great, making the end of slavery an object of the war would surely prevent foreign intervention of any kind.

Those issues, and perhaps his personal feeling, prompted Lincoln to present the matter to the entire Cabinet around August 1. He did not ask for opinions, saying that he had decided the matter and that "we must change our tactics or lose the game." The Secretaries offered some suggestions as to the wording, but then Stanton pointed out that to issue such a radical action while the war was going so badly would seem a desperate act. Stanton suggested that he wait until he "could give it to the country supported by a military success."

Abraham Lincoln. Library of Congress

warning the "states then in rebellion" that if they did not lay down their arms and return to the Union by January 1, 1863, the slaves in those states would be declared "forever free."

That warning was ignored, as expected. At 11 AM on New Year's Day the President hosted a public reception in the Blue Room. When it ended at 2 PM, after shaking many hands, Lincoln retired to his office to officially sign his Emancipation Proclamation. There is an unconfirmed story that as he flexed his tired hand, he remarked that if his signature was shaky, history would say that he hesitated. Although, he preferred signing "A. Lincoln," The Emancipation Proclamation is signed, in a bold hand, "Abraham Lincoln." That document says, in part:

....Now, therefore, I, Abraham Lincoln, President of the United States, by virtue of the power in me vested as Commander-In-Chief of the Army and Navy of the United States in time of actual armed rebellion against the authority and government of the United States, and as a fit and necessary war measure for suppressing said rebellion, do, on this 1st day of January, A.D. 1863, and in accordance with my purpose so to do ... I do order and declare that all persons held as slaves within said designated States and parts of States are, and henceforward shall be, free; and that the Executive Government of the United States, including the military and naval authorities thereof, will recognize and maintain the freedom of said persons....

Lincoln agreed, pocketed the document and made no mention of the subject until after the battle at Antietam near Sharpsburg, Maryland on September 17, 1862. That action was far from a ringing Union victory, but General McClellan's army did manage to force General Lee to abandon his plan to invade Maryland. Lincoln deemed that close enough to victory to make his move. On the 22nd, he called the Cabinet together and said, "Gentlemen, I have, as you are aware, thought a great deal about the relation of this war to slavery.... I made a promise to my self," here Mr. Lincoln hesitated a moment before adding, "and to my Maker. The Rebel army is now driven out and I am going to fulfill that promise." Again, he asked for no advice, merely read the document he had prepared and called for suggestions. The Cabinet approved of what he had written, offering only minor changes. Accordingly, that afternoon, a preliminary proclamation was released

The immediate impact on slavery was, of course, slight. But the political and far reaching effects are a major part of American history. Billy Herndon says that his partner signed that document fully aware of the "responsibilities and magnitude of the act." Herndon also declares that Lincoln told him that issuing the proclamation was, "the central act of my administration and the great event of the nineteenth century." Who could disagree? The man saw something that needed doing, realized that he was in a position to do it and had the courage to act.

Gettysburg

In the summer of 1863, General Lee decided to invade the North once again, this time moving into Pennsylvania where he collided with General George Meade's Union army near the little town of Gettysburg. In fierce fighting on the first three days of July, about 75,000 Confederates battled nearly 100,000 Yankee soldiers. When the smoke cleared, almost 28,000 Americans were wounded and nearly 8,000 – three times the town's population – men of both armies lay dead on the fertile green fields surrounding the tiny town.

Combined with the horses killed, the dead men created a massive burial chore after the armies withdrew. As it was a hot summer in Southern Pennsylvania, the need to cover the bodies was urgent, so many were quickly consigned to shallow graves. As the rains and wind uncovered those hasty interments, a group of local citizens, headed by David Wills, launched a project to purchase some ground on the battlefield adjoining the local cemetery and establish a proper burial ground for the Union dead. Some state support arrived and funds were also supplied for the gristly chore of disinterring and reburial of the hastily buried corpses. Eventually, the committee consisted of members from all the states whose troops had participated in the battle.

When the project was nearly complete, the citizens involved began to think about a dedication ceremony. The date was set for October 3, 1863. America's most famous orator, Edward Everett, was invited to address the crowd which would surely gather. That gentleman replied that he'd be happy to speak at the ceremony, but he could not possibly be ready by the given date. So, the dedication ceremony was postponed by nearly a month, to November 19.

As a matter of courtesy, the Gettysburg committee also invited the President, his Cabinet, the commander of the Union Army that fought there, General George Meade, America's diplomatic corps, foreign representative, members of Congress and other distinguished persons.

Above and at left: *The Gettysburg train depot looks much the same as when President Lincoln arrived there November 18, 1863.*

The Soldiers National Monument marks the spot from which Lincoln delivered his immortal two minute address.

Despite the short notice, Lincoln accepted. On November 18, although he was ill, he, in company with Secretary Stanton, secretaries Nicolay and Hay and a few others boarded a special train for Gettysburg. A persistent story has Lincoln crafting the speech on the train, writing on the back of an envelope, but aside from the fact it is evident that such a masterpiece was not simply dashed off, several drafts have been located. While he may have added some finishing touches on the trip or overnight at Wills' house on the town square, the address was written before he boarded the train.

When Lincoln arrived at the battlefield the next morning to dedicate the cemetery for the fallen soldiers, he was weak, dizzy, and his face "had a ghastly color."

As the saying goes, his "few appropriate remarks," are history. In a mere 272 words, Abraham Lincoln delivered, in about two minutes, the greatest speech of his career, maybe the greatest speech of its kind anyone ever delivered.

The only flaw in it is his gross mistake of thinking that "the world will little note nor long remember what we say here...."

After the invitations were issued, someone in the committee asked, as an afterthought, if it would be appropriate to ask Mr. Lincoln to speak. That issue came in for some hot debate in the committee meeting, but finally the decision was reached to ask Mr. Lincoln "to set apart formally these grounds to their sacred use by a few appropriate remarks" after Mr. Everett's oration. This request went to the White House about November 1.

According to his secretary, on the train back to Washington that evening, Lincoln was feverish and had severe headaches. Then he developed back pains, exhaustion and a widespread scarlet rash that turned blister-like. A servant who attended Lincoln during the three-week illness later developed smallpox and died in January 1864. These

facts have led modern-day doctors to believe that Lincoln may have been suffering with smallpox when he delivered the address.

Like most everything else concerning Lincoln, there is controversy surrounding the Gettysburg speech. Some 15,000 people gathered there had already endured two hours of flowery oration by Mr. Everett before Lincoln stood. His talk was so short that he was finished before many realized he had begun. Therefore, newspaper accounts of what Lincoln actually said vary as to wording and punctuation, as do the five copies that Lincoln wrote out in his own hand in response to requests. Secretaries Nicolay and Hay each received a copy written around the time of the ceremony, one of which may be the actual copy from which Lincoln read that November day. Those two copies are at the Library of Congress. Of the other three, written by Lincoln for charitable purposes, one is in a Springfield museum, and one is privately owned. The other, which is probably the last written by Lincoln, is considered the "official" copy as he signed and dated it, was eventually donated to the American Government provided it be stored at the White House.

The differences are minor, so whichever, if any, is the original matters little in terms of what he actually said. What he did say illustrates, once again, his command of language. Not bad for a sick man with less that one-year's worth of education!

Fort Stevens

Washington, DC, the Capital of the United States and Richmond, Virginia, the Capital of the Confederacy are a scant 100 miles apart. Given that both "eastern" armies operated between the Capitals for most of the war, it is no surprise that both were under constant enemy threat. Cannon fire was heard so often from the White House that Willie and Tad had constructed a fort on the roof.

The fort constructed by the Lincoln boys was just one of many protecting Washington from the never-too-distant Rebels. Another, located on the Seventh Street Pike, now Georgia Avenue, which was the main route into Washington from the north, was named Fort Stevens.

When General U.S. Grant took command in the eastern theater in the spring of 1864, he felt that the nearly 25,000 troops manning the forts guarding Washington could be better utilized in the field, so one of his first moves was to strip the forts of those huge garrisons leaving only about 9000 poorly trained men (mostly home guards, convalescents and clerks) to guard the city. By the summer of 1864, Grant had Lee's Army of Northern Virginia fully occupied defending Richmond. Desperately seeking some way out of the tightening noose, Lee dispatched General Jubal Early with about 20,000 troops to threaten Washington in hopes that Lincoln would order Grant to draw back some of his forces to defend the Capitol. "Old Jube" began his march through the Shenandoah Valley on June 28. Moving quickly, by July 9 Early had surrounded Frederick, Maryland. Sending emissaries into the city, he demanded they pay a $200,000 ransom, or else he would burn every building in town. With that money, plus the $20,000 he got from Hagerstown (he demanded the same $200,000 but somebody dropped a zero) in his pocket, the next day Early camped at Rockville, just north of Washington, having marched about 160 miles in 12 days.

Official Washington went into a panic. Seemingly paralyzed by the threat, action occurred in the city only on orders from Grant, who was 100 miles away at City Point. That gentleman, as usual, had no problem acting and soon had the 25th New York Cavalry and several other infantry units on the way to Fort Stevens.

Had Lee been able to read Grant's telegram, "If the President thinks it advisable that I should go to Washington in person, I can start in an hour after receiving notice, leaving everything here on the defensive," he would have been delighted to see how well his plan was working.

Old Jube knew that Grant would reinforce, so he also knew he was in a footrace. On the morning of July 11, Early reconnoitered the area finding that, although Fort Stevens was supported by similar forts on each side, it was poorly defended and vulnerable. Early's troops spent the afternoon probing for the weakest spot to attack. He thought he could probably take the position by frontal assault, but his men were exhausted and strung out along the road as well. Before his whole force came up, darkness halted the action for the day.

Through the next morning's fog, Early was able to observe that Grant's reinforcements had arrived – he had lost the race. With so many Yankee soldiers there, and

veterans at that, all chance of him taking the fort was gone. Still, his mission was to cause some panic, so he might as well fire a shot or two while he was there.

At the same time, President Lincoln had decided that if he and Secretary Stanton toured the forts, just showing their faces would prove they had not fled and might boost morale. Sometime on the afternoon of July 12, Fort Stevens commander General Horatio Wright bounded out of his underground bunker, on a mission to drive away the Rebel riflemen who had crept with range, to find Lincoln and Stanton approaching his position.

Flustered, no doubt, Wright informed the President of his mission and – inexplicably – asked if he would care to watch, "without for a moment supposing he would accept." The President did care to watch, so he stood on a parapet, where he was in the line of fire. General Wright, wondering why he made such a stupid remark, pleaded, unheard, for him to take cover. At 6'4" and wearing his trademark stove-pipe hat, Lincoln surely made an inviting target for Rebel

sharpshooters as he tranquilly observed the action. After an officer standing within three feet of Lincoln was struck and killed, a young officer shouted at Lincoln, "Get down, you damned fool!" According to Lincoln legend, that officer was none other than Oliver Wendell Holmes, Jr. who would become the distinguished Supreme Court Justice.

Late in the afternoon, Early's forces retreated, leaving 41 Union dead. Those men are buried in Battleground National Cemetery, a few blocks north of Fort Stevens.

Another story connected with the event has it that as Early was marching toward White's Ford on the Potomac, ending his invasion of Maryland, he told his staff, "We

Above: *Fort Stevens, on the outskirts of Washington, where Lincoln was under enemy fire. The rock in the right background marks the spot where the President stood.* **Insert:** *This plaque documents the Commander-in-Chief under fire incident.*

didn't take Washington, but we scared the hell out of Abe Lincoln."

Today Fort Stevens, located at 13th and Quackenbos Streets, NW, off Georgia Avenue in Washington is a National Park Service site where you can go and see one of only two places where America's Commander in Chief came under enemy fire, the other being Bladensburg, Maryland where the British shot at President James Madison during the War of 1812.

Tad

Thomas Lincoln was born in Springfield April 4, 1853, less than two years after his namesake grandfather's death. His father's likening his appearance to a tadpole stuck him with a nickname to last the rest of his short life.

The boy was born with a partially cleft palate, a condition resulting when the two plates that form the roof of the mouth (palate) do not completely join during gestation. As the problem was far beyond the scope of mid-nineteenth century medical science, Tad was left with a marked speech impediment and the requirement that he eat only soft food or other especially prepared items. He was, by most accounts, imaginative, lovable, emotional and exasperating. His personality, coupled with his father's abhorrence of discipline, allowed Tad to become a lovable demon.

In Lincoln's White House, the boys were allowed free range, breaking windows, locking doors, ringing the call bells and often interrupting Cabinet meetings, Capital state dinners, or whatever else might be going on. At the time, the President kept office hours during which he was available to the public. If you desired to see Abe Lincoln, all you had to do was go the White House and get in line. He'd see you when your turn came. But if you didn't want to wait, young Tad would offer to accelerate the process – for a price.

He'd burst into the President's office and announce that he had brought several "friends" to meet his Pa. Tad's having to ask the "friend's" name made Abe suspicious. Investigation revealed that Tad was charging the visitors but contributing the gains to the Sanitary Commission, the Civil War equivalent of the Red Cross. Lincoln suggested that Tad find another way of raising funds.

Lincoln's watch. Courtesy of Kentucky Historical Society Collection.

He did. Washington was thronged with homeless during the war. Some of these simply begged on the government thoroughfares, while others sold fruit. Young Tad would set out in the morning armed with a few dollars and a basket. He'd purchase apples or whatever was in season from the street vendors. Returning to the White House, he'd set up a stand to resell – at a substantial profit – to the Presidential visitors. When Lincoln stopped that enterprise, Tad was hard pressed to understand – he said was helping everyone concerned.

His next scheme interrupted a Cabinet meeting in memorable fashion. During a discussion, Lincoln happened to glance out the window. What he saw caused him to dash wordlessly from the room. Tad was holding perhaps the country's first yard sale, offering – at bargain prices – items he'd gathered from the White House store of china and silverware and his parents' closets.

Most nights, rather than go to bed, Tad would sit up late in the President's office while his father polished off the day's business. When Lincoln was finished, he'd retire to his bedroom, Tad asleep on his shoulder.

Tad was an ardent Union soldier. He and Willie constructed a fort on the White House roof, organized the staff into a sort of home guard battalion and subjected them to regular drill sessions. Secretary of War Stanton authorized him to wear a uniform, complete with saber,

Abraham and Tad Lincoln. Tradition has it that they are viewing a Bible; Bob Lincoln said it was a photograph album. Library of Congress

Inside Ford's Theater, the original decorations still adorn the box where John Wilkes Booth shot the President. Note the bunting on the right, torn when Booth caught his spur as he leapt to the stage.

at the rank of Lieutenant. By all accounts, the young man was a despotic commander.

When Lincoln was shot at Ford's theater, Tad was attending a performance of Aladdin at Grover's Theater. The next morning when Mary Todd returned from the Petersen House and Tad learned that his father was dead, he put his arms around his mother's neck and tried to comfort her, "Don't cry so, Ma! Don't cry, or you will make me cry, too!"

Mary was so stricken with grief after her husband's death that she remained in the White House until May 23, nearly six weeks after the assassination. Finally re-locating in Chicago, she decided to address Tad's nearly illiterate condition. So, he began school in 1866 at age twelve. Soon thereafter, Mary decided to take him to Europe.

From Germany and then England, Mary Lincoln battled Congress for a widow's pension, finally obtaining an annual award of $3000 in 1870. Soon thereafter, she decided to return to America. Tad caught a cold on the ocean trip and was ill when they reached Chicago in mid-May 1871. Within two weeks, he was having difficulty in breathing when lying down and had to sleep sitting up in a chair. Through June and July he was dangerously ill, then better, then worse until finally the pain and agony worsened as his face grew thinner. On Saturday morning, July 15, 1871, Tad Lincoln passed away at the Clifton House in Chicago, He was eighteen years old. The cause of death was not determined but may have been tuberculosis.

Simple funeral services were held for Tad the next day at his brother Robert's home in Chicago. Afterwards, Bob went along as Tad's body was transported to Springfield, their mother too overcome to make the trip. In Springfield more formal funeral services were held at the First Presbyterian Church. Bob said that his brother, although only eighteen "...was so manly and self-reliant that I had the brightest hopes for his future."

Mary Lincoln had now lost a husband and three sons. Small wonder her mental stability was questioned.

The Statue

In the magnificent rotunda beneath our Capitol Dome in Washington D.C. you can see an inspiring white marble statue of Abraham Lincoln placed there six years after his death. The story of how it got there is also inspiring.

In 1862, a young lady named Lavinia (Vinnie) Ream

The exterior of Ford's Theater as it appeared when the Lincoln's attended "Our American Cousin." Library of Congress

Ford's Theater remains unchanged today.

came to Washington to do her part in the war effort. Opportunities for women being what they were in those days, she was fortunate to find work in the Postal Service.

Vinnie was born of humble origins, in Madison, Wisconsin on September 25, 1847. In her early childhood, she displayed a talent for drawing and painting while working with the local Winnebago Indians. When Vinnie was seven, the family moved to Washington, D.C., where she discovered that she also had some talent for modeling in clay. When the family moved to Kansas, Vinnie attended Christian College, a girls' boarding school in Columbia, Missouri where she studied literature, music and, of course, art.

When the family returned to D.C. in 1861, Vinnie

was determined to do her part for the war effort. Despite being female and a teenager, she managed to land a job. In addition, she did volunteer work in the military hospitals, writing letters for wounded soldiers and generally raising morale.

Sometime in 1863, she contacted Missouri Congressman James Rollins hoping to secure funding for a sculpture for Missouri's Christian College. Hence, Vinnie and Rollins came to visit D.C. sculptor Clark Mills' studio. Vinnie watched as Mills continued working while they talked, then she remarked that she could do that, too. Evidently she was right; she was soon apprenticing in Mills' shop in her spare time, sculpting busts of public figures.

The subjects of her work were impressed and wanted

Vinnie with the plaster bust that won her the Government's competition to complete a Lincoln statue. Library of Congress

to support the aspiring young lady. Just who hatched the idea is unclear, but a delegation of Congressmen, headed by Rollins, approached President Lincoln on the young lady's behalf, requesting that he sit for her. Lincoln's flat refusal turned to reluctant acquiescence when Rollins explained that Vinnie, like Lincoln, came from a humble background and was merely trying to improve her lot.

In the fall of 1864, Lincoln was involved in a hot contest for re-election and fairly certain he would lose. He did not, of course, and if you have never read his second inaugural address, you have missed the quintessential example of saying a lot in a few words. Even though he was busy, Lincoln agreed to let Vinnie sit in his office 30 minutes a day while he signed papers and performed other office chores. In his office over the next five months, she studied the President's face and sketched. Only his death at Ford's Theater ended the sessions.

Within a year, Congress opened a competition for a commission to create a full-sized marble statue of Lincoln. Vinnie Ream, "still under the spell of his kind eyes and genial presence" and despite her age and gender, entered the competition. The bust she created won her not only the competition but the admiration of all who saw it. Accordingly, on August 30, 1866, the nineteen-year-old sculptress was awarded a Government contract calling for payment of $5000 upon acceptance of her plaster model and an additional $5000 when she completed the marble statue. That contract made her the first woman (and probably the youngest of any gender) to be awarded a commission to execute a statue for the Government.

For measurements for the plaster model, she was allowed to use the clothes Mr. Lincoln was wearing the night he was killed. Those clothes, incidentally, are currently in the news as they have been removed from display in Ford's Theater while the building is being renovated. In the process of packing them for storage, it has been discovered that Abe Lincoln wore a size fourteen shoe.

In 1869 with Secretary of State William Seward's letter of introduction in her hand, Vinnie went to Italy to select the marble for her statue. She selected pure white marble from Cararra, supposedly the supplier of Michelangelo's favorite medium. Perhaps hoping for inspiration, she decided to remain there to complete the work. Two years later, the statue finished, she returned with it to this country.

On a snowy night in 1871, Lincoln's old pillow fighting companion, Judge David Davis, unveiled Vinnie's work beneath the Capitol Dome in front of a huge crowd. The statue portrays Lincoln standing with his head tilted slightly forward. As you stand in front of the figure, you notice that his eyes are fixed on you and his right arm is extended, handing you his Emancipation Proclamation.

What the statute inspires in each of us, you need to go to the Capitol to experience for yourself. But, the comment Wisconsin Senator Matthew Carpenter uttered at the unveiling gives us an idea of what at least one of President Lincoln's contemporaries thought. "Of this statue, as a mere work of art, I am no judge. What Praxiteles might have thought of such a work, I neither know nor care; but I am able to say, in the presence of this vast and brilliant assembly, that it is Abraham Lincoln all over."

Vinnie Ream's Lincoln statue in the National Capitol Rotunda. The eyes of this effigy are truly captivating.

Springfield
1865 – Forever

"I desire so to conduct the affairs of this administration that if at the end, when I come to lay down the reins of power, I have lost every other friend on earth, I shall at least have one friend left, and that friend shall be down inside of me"

–Abraham Lincoln

Before Abraham Lincoln's body was cold in Washington D.C., two things happened in Springfield, Illinois. For one thing, Billy Herndon started interviewing people and collecting documents for his Lincoln biography.

The other was that the city fathers began plotting to ensure that the slain President would be buried in their city. Mary Lincoln was so prostrate with grief that the burden of dealing with Lincoln's affairs fell on Bob. The President had died intestate, so Bob appealed to his father's old friend, Judge David Davis, for help. Davis was happy to come to Washington to deal with the issues. When these two gentlemen, along with others, agreed that Lincoln should be buried in Springfield, Mrs. Lincoln gave up her insistence that he rest in Chicago or maybe Washington. There is no truth, incidentally, in the persistent rumor that President Lincoln died a poor man. After everything was paid, each of his three heirs received almost $37,000.

Mr. Lincoln died on Saturday morning, April 15, 1865. On that same day, the National Lincoln Monument Association was formed in Springfield to raise funds to erect a tomb to hold his remains. Almost immediately, money poured in from veterans groups, school children and fraternal societies. On Wednesday, April 19 the official funeral was conducted in the East Room of the White House with an Illinois delegation some 400 strong in attendance. However politically incorrect the action may have been, this group descended on Bob Lincoln to lobby with his mother for a Springfield burial. Mary Lincoln

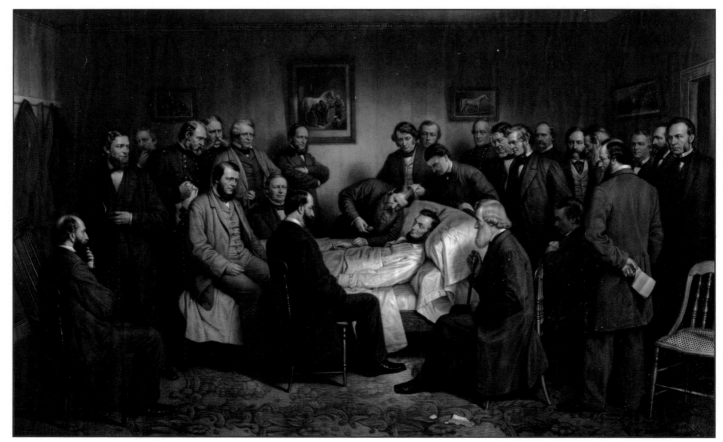

The scene at Lincoln's death on the morning of April 15, 1865, drawn after the fact, compresses the events since the time that he was carried across the street to the Petersen House the previous evening. Although many of the Cabinet Members, Mrs. Lincoln and Robert and Vice-President Johnson were present at various times, accounts indicate that they were not all in the room at the same time.

After seventeen moves, Abraham Lincoln's casket finally came to eternal rest beneath the Memorial in Springfield. The remains of Mary Todd Lincoln and sons Eddie, Willie and Tad also rest inside.

finally agreed, providing that her husband rest in that city's Oak Ridge Cemetery. The delegation did not tell her that a plot in downtown Springfield had already been purchased for his tomb.

After the White House funeral the body was transported to the Capitol where it lay in state the next day as thousands filed by to pay their final respects. On Friday, the casket was loaded, along with Willie's exhumed coffin, on a special train – draped in black cloth with Lincoln's picture above the cowcatcher – at the Baltimore and Ohio station. The long winding journey back to Springfield was, in essence, a reversal of the route Lincoln had traveled four years earlier. Some kind of memorial service – some more elaborate than others – was held at every stop. Bob Lincoln was among some three hundred mourners who left Washington on the train, but he traveled only to Baltimore before returning to his grieving mother.

A mourning public lined the tracks for almost the entire 1700 mile journey, braving the spring rains with bared heads. Incidentally, Mr. Lincoln's ghost not only haunts the White House and his Springfield home, but the funeral train has been seen along the same route several times since 1865.

Finally, the train pulled into the Chicago and Alton depot on Jefferson Street in Springfield early on May 3. Mr. Lincoln's body would lie in state in the Hall of Representatives – the very room in which he gave his famous "House Divided" speech – in the State House across from his law office that day. Mr. Lincoln's face had become discolored, so an undertaker, using rouge chalk and amber, restored the face to near normal color.

May 4 was a hot day in Springfield. At 10:00 A.M. the doors to the State House were closed to keep the public out while Mr. Lincoln's body was prepared for burial by the undertaker and embalmer. An elegant gold, silver, and crystal hearse loaned by the city of St. Louis carried the coffin along a winding route past Mr. Lincoln's home, past the Governor's Mansion, and finally to Oak Ridge Cemetery. The procession was led by Major General Joseph Hooker, one of the men whom Lincoln had put in command of the Union Army. Lincoln's personal horse, Old Bob, wearing a mourning blanket followed immediately behind the hearse. Only Mr. Lincoln's son, Bob, and his rail-splitting cousin, John Hanks represented the immediate family. Upon arrival

at the cemetery, Lincoln's coffin, along with Willie's, was placed in a receiving vault.

In December, with the tomb under construction, the two bodies along with Eddie's which had been exhumed, were moved to a temporary vault, the location of which is today marked with a small granite marker on the hill behind the tomb. By the time Tad died in 1871, the memorial was complete enough for use, so the youngest son was the first to occupy the tomb. Soon, Lincoln and the other two sons joined Tad inside the memorial. When the memorial, constructed of marble from five states and four foreign countries and statuary made from Civil War cannons, was completed in 1874, Lincoln's body was moved once again, this time to a marble sarcophagus in the burial chamber inside the tomb. All hoped he'd come to the eternal rest he so richly deserves.

Not yet. In 1876, a gang of Illinois counterfeiters hatched an insane plot to steal Lincoln's corpse from the tomb to hold it for ransom. They expected to gain $200,000 and the release of their master engraver who was incarcerated at Joliet State prison.

Whatever chance the scheme had of working disappeared when one of the conspirators got drunk in a Springfield bar and revealed the plan while trying to impress a woman. Soon, the fledgling Secret Service was in on the proposed action.

Thinking that the city would be too busy on election night to notice a little grave robbery, the action was scheduled for November 7. In the darkest part of the night, part of the gang approached the tomb, broke the padlock on the iron door and moved into the burial chamber while the others waited outside. Unknown to all of the gang except the one who was actually a secret service agent, eight agents were hiding nearby. As the men pushed the marble lid of the sarcophagus aside and attempted to lift the coffin out, the agent made his prearranged signal to the men outside. Despite the ineptitude demonstrated so far, the gang evidently detected something amiss and exited the tomb before the armed detectives could rush in. Although the grave robbers escaped that night, they were arrested a short time later in Chicago and soon joined their master engraver at Joliet.

Following that incident, Lincoln's body was moved, once again, to a secret location within the memorial. When Mary Lincoln died in 1882, her remains were placed beside her husband's in the hidden location. In 1887, both caskets were moved to a more secure location in a brick vault constructed beneath the burial room. The marble sarcophagus remained in place above them and visitors never suspected they were viewing an empty box.

In 1895, the foundation which had raised the money to build the memorial deeded the 12.5 acres of land and the memorial itself to the State of Illinois. As the entire structure was in need of repair, a renovation program was undertaken beginning in 1899. At that time, all six caskets (Abe, Mary, their three boys and Bob's son Jack) were moved to a subterranean vault elsewhere in the cemetery. When the renovation was finished in August 1901, the caskets were moved back into the memorial, Lincoln's being placed in the sarcophagus where it had been when the attempted robbery occurred back in '76.

That arrangement did not sit well with Bob Lincoln, so in September, he decided to move his father's remains one final time – at his own expense – this time to a very secure location. A ten foot deep pit was dug beneath the burial chamber where the coffin would be placed in a steel cage and then covered with concrete.

Before that happened, a discussion came up concerning some persistent rumors. Ideas such as the grave robbers had switched the contents of the coffin and that Lincoln was never actually in that coffin in the first place kept cropping up despite the fact that such things were known to be nonsense as the casket had already been opened four times during the various moves. This burial action, however, was to be final, so the decision was reached to open the casket once again to verify that Abraham Lincoln's remains were, indeed, inside. An oval opening was cut in the lead lined coffin to expose the corpse's head and shoulders. Lincoln's body had been embalmed so many times on the journey back to Springfield that, even though he'd been dead for thirty-five years, the body was not decomposed at all. All twenty-three people who viewed the remains that day identified the body and agreed that Abraham Lincoln was indeed the corpse in the casket.

The part of the casket removed for the opening was soldered back in place, the casket was placed inside the cage and lowered into the pit. More than 4000 pounds of concrete then sealed the final resting place.

So, on September 26, 1901, more than thirty-five years after that tragic night in Ford's Theater and seventeen moves from one place to another, Abraham Lincoln was finally allowed the eternal rest that he deserves as much as or more than anyone else who ever lived.

There are lives to be envied and there are lives to be admired. Not many of us would envy the tragic and heartbreaking life of Abraham Lincoln. But, who among us can fail to admire one of the greatest Americans of all time?

Lincoln through the darkness. The statue is designed to suggest that Lincoln is about to stand. This view enhances that impression.

Bibliography

Angle, Paul M., ed, *The Lincoln Reader*, Rutgers University Press, New Brunswick, NJ, 1947

Basler, Roy P. Ed., *Collected Works of Abraham Lincoln*, Rutgers University Press, New Brunswick, NJ, 1959

Bassett, Margaret, *Abraham and Mary Todd Lincoln*, Thomas Y Crowell Company, New York, 1973

Clay, Cassius M, *The Life, Memoirs, Writing and Speeches of Cassius M. Clay*, J. Fletcher Brennan & Co., Cincinnati, OH 1886

Current, Richard N., *The Lincoln Nobody Knows*, McGraw-Hill Book Company, New York, 1958.

Dirck, Brian, *Lincoln the Lawyer*, University of Illinois Press, Urbana, IL, 2007.

Foote, Shelby, *The Civil War A Narrative*, Vintage Books, New York, 1958

Goff, John S., *Robert Todd Lincoln A Man in his Own Right*, University of Oklahoma Press, Norman, OK, 1969

Goodwin, Doris Kerns, *Team of Rivals*, Simon and Schuster, New York, 2005

Harrison, Lowell H., *Lincoln of Kentucky*, University Press of Kentucky, Lexington, KY 2000.

Helm, Katherine, *The True Story of Mary, Wife of Lincoln*, Harper & Brothers Publishers, New York, 1918

Herndon, William H. and Weik, Jesse W., *Herndon's Lincoln: The True Story of a Great Life*, 3 vols, Belford, Clarke & Co., Chicago, 1889

Louisville Courier-Journal, various issues 1868 - 2007

Nicolay, John and Hay, John, *Abraham Lincoln, A History*, 10 vols, The Century Company, New York 1890.

Original papers in the case of *Commonwealth of Kentucky v Abraham Lincoln, 1853*. Kentucky State Archives, Frankfort, KY.

Original Lincoln documents stored at the Library of Congress are available on line at http://memory.loc.gov/ammem/alhtml/malhome.html

Remini, Robert V., *Henry Clay, Statesman for the Union*, W.W. Norton Company, New York, NY, 1991

Sandberg, Carl, *Abraham Lincoln, The Prairie Years*, Harcourt Brace Jovanovich, New York, NY, 1926

Tarbell, Ida M., *The Life of Abraham Lincoln*, McClure, Phillips and Company, New York, 1900.

Townsend, William, *Lincoln and His Wife's Hometown*, Bobbs-Merrill Company, Indianapolis, 1929.

Wilson, Douglas L., *Lincoln Before Washington*, University of Illinois Press, Urbana, IL, 1997

Wilson, Douglas L. and Rodney O Davis, ed. *Herndon's Informants*, University of Illinois Press, Urbana, IL, 1998

Ron Elliott

John W. Snell

Ron Elliott, a native of Lincoln County, Kentucky, is a graduate of Stanford High School, Eastern Kentucky University and the University of Kentucky with degrees in math and computer science.

Ron's background includes involvement with the historic Apollo missions which placed Americans on the moon and a stint on the faculty in Kentucky's Community College system. A history buff from childhood, his interest in history was heightened by having a relative involved in the assassination of Kentucky's 1900 would-be governor, William Goebel.

Mr. Elliott's story-telling ability and wealth of knowledge make him a popular speaker for literature classes, writing seminars, genealogical workshops and historical society meetings. Coupling those attributes with his remarkable research skills and a witty writing style produces well-accepted books. He has mastered the art of presenting historic stories in an extremely readable format giving the reader the "you are there" feeling. Ron is the author of *Assassination at the State House, The Silent Brigade, Inside the Beverly Hills Supper Club Fire* and numerous magazine articles in such prestigious publications as *The Filson History Quarterly*.

Semi-retired, Ron and his wife, Carol, currently live in Nelson County, Kentucky.

In late 2000, following an 18-year stint as the computing center director at Transylvania University in Lexington, Kentucky, John W. Snell began his pursuit of a long-time dream of a career in photography. By 2006, his success in landscape and nature photography led him to partner with Acclaim Press to author *Red River Gorge, The Eloquent Landscape*, a book containing 130 of his color photographs. The book, released in November, 2006, garnered high praise and quickly went into a second printing. When Acclaim needed a photographer for *Through the Eyes of Lincoln*, they immediately looked to Kentucky native John W. Snell to provide the modern day photographic images for the book.

Snell's work has appeared in *Outdoor Photographer, Popular Photography & Imaging* and *Keeneland* magazines. He has won honors for his photography in various Lexington Art League and Creative Camera Club (based in Lexington) competitions. He is a juried member of Kentucky Crafted: The Market and The Kentucky Guild of Artists and Craftsmen, and participates in a variety of juried art fairs. His work is sold in galleries throughout Kentucky, and his prints hang in offices and residential walls as far away as Australia. A guest speaker at Kentucky state park photography weekends, he also teaches photography workshops for the Lexington Art League. He lives in Lexington, Kentucky with his wife, Anne.

Archival quality photographic prints of the color images contained in this book may be purchased directly from John W. Snell. For more information on these and other images, you may contact him via e-mail (john@johnsnellphoto.com), phone (toll-free 1-888-310-4560) or visit his website (www.johnsnellphoto.com).

INDEX